Clausewitz: A Very Short Introduction

'As a synthesis of Clausewitz scholarship this study can
hardly be faulted.'
English Historical Review

VERY SHORT INTRODUCTIONS are for anyone wanting a stimulating and accessible way into a new subject. They are written by experts, and have been translated into more than 45 different languages.

The series began in 1995, and now covers a wide variety of topics in every discipline. The VSI library now contains over 500 volumes—a Very Short Introduction to everything from Psychology and Philosophy of Science to American History and Relativity—and continues to grow in every subject area.

Titles in the series include the following:

Michael Howard

CLAUSEWITZ

A Very Short Introduction

OXFORD
UNIVERSITY PRESS

OXFORD
UNIVERSITY PRESS

Great Clarendon Street, Oxford OX2 6DP

Oxford University Press is a department of the University of Oxford.
It furthers the University's objective of excellence in research, scholarship,
and education by publishing worldwide in

Oxford New York

Auckland Bangkok Buenos Aires Cape Town Chennai
Dar es Salaam Delhi Hong Kong Istanbul Karachi Kolkata
Kuala Lumpur Madrid Melbourne Mexico City Mumbai Nairobi
São Paulo Shanghai Taipei Tokyo Toronto

Oxford is a registered trade mark of Oxford University Press
in the UK and in certain other countries

Published in the United States
by Oxford University Press Inc., New York

© Michael Howard 1983, 2002

British Library Cataloguing in Publication Data
Data available

Library of Congress Cataloging in Publication Data
Data available

ISBN 978-0-19-280257-6

19 20

Typeset by RefineCatch Ltd, Bungay, Suffolk
Printed in Great Britain by
Ashford Colour Press Ltd, Gosport, Hants.

Contents

Note on quotations

Bracketed arabic numerals refer to the pages of Karl von Clausewitz *On War*, ed. and trans. Michael Howard and Peter Paret. Copyright © 1976 by Princeton University Press. Excerpts reprinted by permission of Princeton University Press. The quotations on p. 16 and on p. 36 line 19 are translated from *Bemerkungen über die reine und angewandte Strategie des Herrn von Bülow*, 1805, reprinted in *Verstreute Kleine Schriften*, 68, 77 and 69, and from *Strategie aus dem Jahre 1804*, ibid. 20. The quotation from a letter given on p. 18 is taken from Peter Paret, *Clausewitz and the State*, 129. The definition on p. 36 is translated from *Strategie aus dem Jahre 1804* in *Verstreute Kleine Schriften*, 33. Bibliographical details of all these works are given in the Further Reading section at the end of the book.

Karl von Clausewitz, engraving c.1800. *Hulton Archive*.

Introduction

About Karl von Clausewitz's study *On War* the American strategic thinker Bernard Brodie has made the bold statement 'His is not simply the greatest, but the only great book about war.' It is difficult to disagree. Anyone trying to put together a collection of texts on military theory comparable to anthologies on social, political, or economic thought will find it hard to match Clausewitz. Few if any other writers on war have succeeded as he did in transcending the limitations imposed on their insights by the political or the technological circumstances of their times. We can find many whose writings illustrate how successive generations have thought about war, but there are remarkably few who can help us to think about it; who have penetrated below the ephemeral phenomena of their own times and considered war, not just as a craft, but as a great socio-political activity, distinguished from all other activities by the reciprocal and legitimized use of purposeful violence to attain political objectives. There is certainly the magisterial study by Sun Tzu: *The Art of War*, probably written in the fourth century BC. There are a few chapters in the works of Clausewitz's contemporary Jomini; there are passages scattered among the works of Liddell Hart and his eccentric contemporary J. F. C. Fuller; and there are many interesting insights to be excavated from the writings of Marx, Engels, Lenin, and Trotsky. Among earlier writers one can glean much bleak wisdom from the *obiter dicta* of Thucydides and Machiavelli. But there is no systematic study comparable to that of Clausewitz. Military analysts are usually concerned rather to advise their own generations and their own societies than to distil lasting wisdom for posterity.

Clausewitz expressed the modest hope that his book would not be forgotten after two or three years, and 'might be picked up more than once by those who are interested in the subject' (p. 63). But his main concern was to help his countrymen and his contemporaries. He was a member of the Prussian officer corps, loyal to the Hohenzollern dynasty though more conscious than most of the problems it faced in coming to terms with the political currents set in motion by the French Revolution. He believed that the menace of French aggression had been checked by the European powers in 1814–15 but by no means destroyed, and if he sought to understand war in the abstract it was only to ensure that in future Prussia and her allies would be able to wage it more swiftly and effectively against the hereditary foe. Above all he was a professional soldier writing for his professional colleagues, not an academic lecturing in a political science faculty. He quite deliberately limited his analysis to what was likely to be of immediate utility to a commander planning a campaign. He had the practical man's horror of abstractions that could not be directly related to the facts of the situation, of propositions that could not be illustrated by examples, of material that was not relevant to the problem in hand. Certainly as a thinker he sought to penetrate to the essence of his subject-matter. But he was always concerned to link theory to action, and he deliberately ignored all aspects of his subject that were not of immediate relevance to the conduct of the kind of war with which he himself was familiar.

> The conduct of war [*he wrote*] has nothing to do with making guns and powder out of coal, sulphur, saltpetre, copper and tin; its given quantities are weapons that are ready for use and their effectiveness. Strategy uses maps without worrying about trigonometrical surveys; it does not enquire how a country should be organised and a people trained and ruled in order to produce the best military results. It takes these matters as it finds them in the European community of nations . . . (p. 144)

2

To that extent, therefore, Clausewitz deliberately sacrificed universality to pragmatism and simplicity. It may however be doubted whether he was conscious of quite how much he was sacrificing. It is easy enough, after two World Wars, to criticize a theory of war that excluded all consideration of the economic base that makes the fighting of war possible at all, but to do this is not just to evoke the wisdom of hindsight. It demanded a very narrow view of the nature of war to study the Napoleonic period so intensively as did Clausewitz without taking into account the part played in Napoleon's strategy, and perhaps in his downfall, by the Continental System – his attempt to use economic as well as military instruments to consolidate and extend his conquests. Clausewitz's ignorance of the whole maritime dimension of warfare is striking but not surprising. The oceans lay beyond his cultural horizons. It is more curious that a Prussian specialist on military questions, whose country had been established as a major military power as much through skill in economic management as by military victories, should virtually ignore a dimension of military affairs that had occupied the fore-front of the mind of every Prussian soldier, statesman and bourgeois since the days of Frederick William I. Perhaps this one-sidedness reflected the limitations of Clausewitz's own personality and interests. More probably it was the impact of the great Napoleonic campaigns that shaped his career and dominated his thinking – campaigns whose dramatic course and cataclysmic results over-shadowed the humdrum concerns of military budgeting and administration that had so obsessed the old Prussian army. When it came to the point, it was the successful conduct of operations that mattered, and the events of Clausewitz's lifetime had made it clear that it was to this, and not to the deeper questions relating to military financing, budgeting, procurement, and administration, that attention had most urgently to be given.

Clausewitz's ignoring of the economic dimension of war was thus, at least in part, deliberate. His ignoring of another dimension, the technological, was unconscious, and more easily understandable. Like most of his intelligent contemporaries he realized very well that he had been born into a revolutionary era likely to transform, for better or worse, the entire political structure of European society. But no more than anyone else could he appreciate that he was living on the eve of a technological transformation of yet vaster scope. The conduct of war is determined above all by two factors: the nature of the weapons available and the modes of transportation. The first had remained stable for a hundred years, the second for a thousand. In Clausewitz's day as in Caesar's, logistics were determined by the speed and endurance of marching men and of draught animals. Tactics were determined, as they had been in the age of Marlborough, by firearms whose effective range was 50 yards and cannon with a range of 300; and although there had been significant incremental developments during the past century, developments whose significance Clausewitz analyses most interestingly in the course of *On War*, there was no reason to expect the transformation, both in transportation and in armaments, that began in the decade following Clausewitz's death in 1831 with the development of railways and the introduction of breech-loading rifled firearms.

Much of On *War* is therefore of interest only to military historians, dealing as it does with detailed questions of tactics and logistics that were to be out of date within a few decades of Clausewitz's death. What is remarkable, however, is how much of what Clausewitz had to say did outlast his time and remain relevant, not only under military circumstances transformed out of all recognition, but for a readership far broader than the officers of the Prussian Army whose education he primarily had in mind. Why this should be so it will be the purpose of this volume to explain.

Chapter 1
Clausewitz in his time

The active career of Karl von Clausewitz exactly spanned the course of the Revolutionary and Napoleonic Wars between 1792 and 1815. He was born in 1780, the son of a half-pay lieutenant in the Prussian Army, and at the age of 12 obtained a commission in the 34th Infantry Regiment, which was at the time commanded by a distant relative. But his family was not a military, much less an aristocratic one. His father, whose own forebears had been bourgeois and academic, had been commissioned by Frederick the Great only during the crisis period of the Seven Years War when the exclusive barriers of the Prussian officer corps had been reluctantly lowered to admit members of the middle classes; and he had been retired after that war not, as he and his family gave out, as a result of wounds received on active service, but in consequence of Frederick's reduction of the officer corps to its original nucleus of well-born landed gentry (*Junkers*). Thus although Clausewitz passed his life as a member of that exclusive body, and was even to gain entry into the entourage of the royal family, he was temperamentally an outsider; and the way in which he was ultimately treated by Frederick William III and his court suggests that he was seen as such.

Clausewitz was always something of an introvert; solitary, bookish, shy, intellectually arrogant. An autodidact, he devoured literature on any available topic, not only military affairs but philosophy, politics, art, and education. He was a prolific, almost a compulsive writer on all these matters; from the age of 20 until his death in 1831, his writing was only briefly interrupted by the demands of military campaigning, and no complete edition of his work has ever been compiled. But beneath the scholarly, withdrawn exterior there burned an ambition for military glory worthy of Stendhal's Julien Sorel: an ambition deeply repressed, given vent only in his letters to his wife; never to be fulfilled in the series of staff appointments for which his superiors considered, probably rightly, that his intellectual talents best fitted him; but one that gave a peculiar intensity to his analyses of the qualities demanded of a commander in the field, of the intense moral pressures that commanders must learn to withstand, and of the bloody drama of battle that was the natural, indeed the desirable, climax of all his endeavours. All Clausewitz's writings bear the stamp of a passionate temperament, as often at war with as in the service of a powerful analytic mind.

Clausewitz was no desk soldier. He received his baptism of fire at the age of 13, when the Prussian Army, on the left wing of the forces of the First Coalition containing and driving back the armies of the First French Republic, was campaigning first on the Rhine, then in the Vosges. Advancing across that broad valley, trudging up and down those steep, wooded mountain tracks, he acquired that infantryman's familiarity with terrain that was to inspire so many of the pages of *On War*.

The campaign ended with the Treaty of Basel in 1795, and Prussia withdrew into a precarious and self-deluding state of 'non-alignment' from which she was to be cruelly aroused eleven years later. The first five years of this period was spent by Clausewitz on garrison duty in the small town of Neuruppin. Intelligent soldiers never waste the long periods of leisure that characterize peacetime service. Clausewitz made good use of the excellent library of Frederick the Great's brother Prince Henry, which was open to the officers of his regiment, and he acquired a deep practical interest in education: activities, it may be assumed, that did not engage the interests of his fellow subalterns quite so profoundly. It must nevertheless have come as something of a relief when in 1801 he was transferred to Berlin to attend the newly opened War College under the direction of Gerd von Scharnhorst. It was now, at the age of 19, that his career really began.

Scharnhorst is rightly revered as one of the giants in the creation of Germany, a man as distinguished as a thinker and a statesman as he was as a soldier. A Hanoverian by birth and an artilleryman by training – two characteristics that set him apart from the *Junker* cavalry and infantry officers who dominated the Prussian Army – his brilliant performance in the War of the First Coalition gained for him universal respect, and his appointment as director of the first Prussian staff college was remarkably wise. From the beginning of the wars he had been puzzling over the performance of the French revolutionary armies. How was it that this rabble, untrained, undisciplined, under-officered, its generals as often as not jumped-up NCOs, with no adequate supply system let alone any serious administrative structure, how did it come about that these remarkable forces could not only hold their own against the professional soldiers of the European powers but actually defeat them? It was true that the French made ingenious use of the new flexible and dispersed infantry formations which the Royal Army had been developing before the revolution, and that in the *matériel*, the tactics, and the training of their artillery they were second to none. But the reasons for their military success lay deeper than that. The success of the French armies, Scharnhorst discerned, was closely connected with the transformation of the society that lay behind them, with the emergence of the idea of a French Nation. To learn how to defeat the French it was not enough just to study their military techniques, essential though this might be. One had to consider the political context as well, and the historical background against which these techniques had emerged. The syllabus of the Kriegsakademie was thus liberal as well as technical, and Scharnhorst supplemented it with a discussion group, the Militärische Gesellschaft, where no limit was observed in considering the implications of the military revolution of the time.

This was the setting in which the young Clausewitz now found himself, and he quickly attached himself to Scharnhorst as a deeply admiring disciple, his own ideas germinating and sprouting in the rays of that genial sun. Scharnhorst reciprocated with an equal affection for the brilliant and receptive young man. The foundation was laid for a partnership that was to end only with Scharnhorst's premature death in 1813 and was to bring Clausewitz into the heart of the group of military reformers – Grolman, Boyen, Gneisenau among others – who were to remould the Prussian army and work towards the remaking of the Prussian state. But the opportunity for this still lay in the future, and Clausewitz's immediate prospects, though glittering, were more orthodox. Graduating at the head of his class in 1803, he was appointed adjutant to Prince August, the son of his regiment's colonel-in-chief Prince Ferdinand, and at the end of the year, in the house of his patron, he met and fell in love with Marie, daughter of the Count von Brühl, a lively and well-educated girl high in the favour of Queen Louise. The family's resistance to this unsuitable match and the demands of military service delayed the marriage for seven years, which made possible the long, passionate, self-revealing correspondence in which Clausewitz developed many of his ideas. Once married, Marie was to identify herself wholeheartedly with her husband's work, act as his amanuensis and after his death as his editor, and preside over what still remains the most complete edition of his works which she published in 1832–4.

During the next two years, 1803–5, Clausewitz wrote prolifically, developing ideas that were to receive their final form twenty years later when he came to write *On War*. Then in 1806 came the war with France that the cautious King Frederick William III had done his best to avoid, but to which Clausewitz, like most other patriotic young officers, looked forward with impatient enthusiasm. His master Prince August was given command of a battalion, and Clausewitz accompanied him to the battlefield of Auerstadt. There he participated in his first great Napoleonic battle and in the catastrophic retreat that followed; an experience so shatteringly different from the tedious marches and manœuvres of his boyhood that it was hard for him to comprehend them both as belonging to the single activity, war. He and Prince August were eventually cut off and taken prisoner. While Scharnhorst and his colleagues were retrieving the reputation of the Prussian Army in the Eylau campaign the following year, Clausewitz languished in bitter if not uncomfortable exile with his royal master in France, until they were repatriated after the Peace of Tilsit in 1808. It was a humiliating experience that stoked the fires of Clausewitz's patriotic zeal and gave him a lifelong dislike for all things French.

Released from captivity, Clausewitz rejoined Scharnhorst, who was now in Königsberg, remote from the French-dominated capital of Berlin, working to reorganize the Prussian Army. For the next four years he helped with the task of reshaping the structure of Prussian military institutions, simultaneously writing on every conceivable aspect of his subject, from the details of minor tactics to the problems of political loyalty. The latter became insoluble for him when in the spring of 1812 the king whose uniform he wore and whose claims on his loyalty he had never questioned concluded an alliance with the French enemy Clausewitz so detested. It was too much. In company with some thirty other officers Clausewitz resigned his commission, parted again from his wife, and took service with Emperor Alexander I of Russia, just as the French and their satellite armies were invading that Empire.

Although Clausewitz spoke no Russian, employment was found for him in various advisory positions on the staff. He took part in his second great battle at Borodino. He witnessed the disastrous crossing of the Beresina by the retreating French army and wrote a horrifying account of it. Finally he acted as an intermediary when in December 1812 the commander of the Prussian corps serving under Napoleon's command, Yorck von Wartenberg, took his historic decision to capitulate at Tauroggen and go over with his forces to the side of the Russians. When Yorck established a centre of Prussian national resistance at Königsberg Clausewitz organized the arming of the population; and when in the spring of 1813 the King of Prussia himself at last abandoned Napoleon Clausewitz returned to Berlin, rejoined Scharnhorst, and again helped him to raise new armies, channelling the enthusiasm and self-sacrifice of the subjects of the Hohenzollerns who were beginning to think of themselves as Germans.

When the campaign of 1813 opened Clausewitz accompanied the army to the field. But he was still denied the position of command he wanted so badly. The King had still not forgiven him for what he saw as his disloyal conduct, and a further year passed before he readmitted Clausewitz to his service. So it was wearing the uniform of a Russian officer that Clausewitz served as adviser to the Prussian Army commander, Marshal Blücher, during the Leipzig campaign. When in 1814 he was at last readmitted to the Prussian Army, he was given command only of a nondescript force, 'the German Legion' serving in north Germany, far from the main battlefields in France. Not until 1815 was he readmitted to the Prussian General Staff and appointed chief of staff to General von Thielmann's III Army Corps. This formation served on the extreme left wing of the Allied forces in Belgium and fought a stubborn defensive action against a force double its size under Marshal Grouchy while Napoleon was trying so unsuccessfully to break through the Allied centre before Waterloo. In its unspectacular role III Corps contributed as much to the Allied victory as any of the troops engaged under Wellington or Blücher, but Clausewitz again felt cheated. He took no part in the pursuit of the defeated French, and his hopes of winning glory on the battlefield faded for good.

Scharnhorst was now dead, but his place both as leader of the reforming wing of the Prussian Army and as Clausewitz's principal patron had been taken by August von Gneisenau, another non-Prussian (he was born in Saxony) in the royal service. Gneisenau was appointed Commander-in-Chief of the Prussian forces in the West, and Clausewitz became his chief of staff. Their headquarters at Mainz acquired in Berlin a reputation for nationalism, if not radicalism, certainly for dangerous independence of thought. First Gneisenau, then in 1813 Clausewitz, were recalled to Berlin, where they could be kept more closely under the royal eye. For Clausewitz a place was found as Director of the War College, the Allgemeine Kriegsschule, but his opportunities there of influencing the political or even the military thinking of the Prussian officer corps were slight. His duties were purely administrative, and after his initial proposals for reform had been rebuffed he made no effort to develop them.

For twelve years he remained undisturbed, writing studies of the Napoleonic campaigns and drafts for the comprehensive study *On War* that he projected as early as 1816. These drafts were still incomplete when, in 1830, Clausewitz was posted, first to the command of a major artillery formation in Breslau, then, when the simultaneous risings in Paris and in Poland made a new war seem probable, as chief of staff to his old chief Gneisenau, now in command of the Prussian Army. The danger of war passed, to be succeeded by one yet more frightening: cholera, spreading from the east. The last task assigned to Clausewitz was to organize a *cordon sanitaire* to check the advance of the epidemic into Germany, but it was a problem his strategic insights could not solve. He himself caught the disease and died within twenty-four hours at Breslau, on 16 November 1831, at the age of 51.

Although he never obtained the independent command for which he longed, Clausewitz enjoyed, like so many officers of his generation, an experience of warfare almost unprecedented in its variety. The army which he joined in 1792 was the small homogeneous professional force of Frederick the Great. That in which he served from 1813 to 1815 (and which he had done so much to create) was a great national army based on compulsory service, powerfully backed up by territorial units of volunteers and by an angry, self-conscious nation. His early experience had been in eighteenth-century campaigns of manœuvre and siege warfare. Before he was 40 he had taken part in some of the greatest battles in the history of warfare and seen the armies of Napoleon storm their way across Europe to Moscow, only to be driven back again with little expectation of permanence. All this had been the result of military operations, but it was clear to Clausewitz as a very young man that the explanation for the success or failure of these operations was not to be sought on the battlefield alone. Military analysis, if it was to be of any practical value to posterity, had to be carried to a deeper level than ever before.

The intellectual background

There had been no lack of effort before Clausewitz's time in applying scientific principles to the conduct of war. Throughout the eighteenth century there was a widespread impatience that, in an age when the universe was yielding more and more of its secrets to scientific enquiry and when reason was replacing custom and superstition as the criterion of human judgement, the conduct of war should still be such a clumsy, wasteful, and uncertain business. 'Every science has principles and rules,' wrote the great eighteenth-century general, Prince Maurice of Saxony, 'only that of War has none.' It was a lack widely lamented among professional soldiers for reasons that I shall consider in a moment, but 'enlightened' civilian thinkers lamented that war should survive at all as a relic of a barbarous past. This opinion was widespread throughout Europe but, for two reasons, it was particularly strong in Prussia.

In the first place the experiences of the Seven Years War (1756–63), when Prussian territory had been repeatedly fought over and the resources of both State and people had been almost exhausted, had created throughout the Prussian intelligentsia a profound aversion to war, not unlike that in France and Britain after the First World War, and one that Frederick the Great did nothing to discourage. He himself had had enough fighting to last him a lifetime. In the second place Frederick deliberately reverted to the military policy of his forebears and eliminated the middle classes from both the officer corps and the ranks of his army, leaving them free to make the money which the Prussian state, so barren of natural resources, so badly needed to maintain its position in Europe. As a result there developed in the Prussian middle classes the impression that the king's wars were nothing to do with them; and from that it was a small step to the belief that, if it were not for the king and the nobility who fought his wars, those wars need never happen at all. Immanuel Kant was only one of the many Prussian writers who from 1780 onwards were arguing that if only the affairs of States were in the hands of rational, humane men, the world might enjoy perpetual peace. It was a view dominant in Prussian university and intellectual circles until the catastrophe of Jena shocked them into political awareness and set on foot the new nationalist movement that was to have such momentous consequences.

Professional military writers naturally did not share these opinions. Nevertheless the belief was becoming widespread that war in the hands of experts could be carried on with such skill and moderation as to be virtually bloodless. Military thinkers sought for rational principles based on hard, quantifiable data that might reduce the conduct of war to a branch of the natural sciences, a rational activity from which the play of chance and uncertainty had been entirely eliminated. For some this data was provided by topographical and geographical measurements, for some by calculations of supply needs and march-tables, for some by the geometrical relationship of supply lines to fighting fronts or of armies to their bases. All believed that, in the words of the Welsh soldier of fortune, Henry Lloyd (1720–83), 'whoever understands these things is in a position to initiate military operations with mathematical precision and to keep on waging war without ever being under the necessity of striking a blow'.

But this search for scientific certainty in military affairs was taking place at a time when thinkers concerned with other areas of human activity were beginning to question the whole idea of scientific certainty, a Newtonian universe whose objective reality was governed by forces and

13

principles quite external to man. The idea of the British philosophers Berkeley and Hume that man did not passively observe and absorb knowledge, but rather by the process of observation created it and moulded the world through his own consciousness, had taken deep hold in Germany. Clausewitz did not need to read the works of his contemporary Kant (and there is no evidence that he did) to become familiar with these ideas which formed the basis of Kant's philosophy. He had also absorbed those that had re-entered philosophical thought with the revival of Hellenism and were so powerfully to influence the work of the young Hegel: the Socratic distinctions between the ideal and its manifestations, between the absolute, unattainable concept and the imperfect approaches to it in the real world. The young Clausewitz would have encountered such ideas as these wherever he turned: in his reading at Neuruppin in the 1790s, at the War College where Kant's pupil Kiesewetter was expounding Kantian philosophy, and in the intellectual circles in which he moved in Berlin. His interest in education brought him in touch with the view of such writers as Pestalozzi that education was not a matter of imparting knowledge but of using knowledge to develop the human personality towards its perfect fulfilment. His studies in aesthetic theory taught him that the artist did not succeed simply by learning and applying a given set of rules, but rather that those rules had significance only as indications of what great artists had actually done, and had to be modified as the innovations and perceptions of new generations enriched the comprehension of their subject. All art, all thought (for as Clausewitz himself expressed it, all thought is art), was a *creative* activity, not an imitative or derivative one. And the same applied with particular force to the conduct of war.

Intellectually Clausewitz was very much a child of his time. For him war was not an activity governed by scientific laws but a clash of wills, or moral forces. The successful commander was not the one who knew the rules of the game, but the one who through his genius created them. The uncertainties and hazards that made war so unpredictable and uncontrollable were not barriers to be eliminated but opportunities to be grasped and exploited. The circumstances of the time might have reduced warfare to a matter of absurd, rococo formality, but in its essence war was something very different. Napoleon had made this clear for all to see; Clausewitz set himself to explain it.

The military background

The army that Clausewitz joined as a boy had been moulded by Frederick the Great, and until its destruction in 1806 none of its leaders saw any reason to change the mould. It was perfectly adapted to the ritual of eighteenth-century warfare – a ritual that was itself determined by the nature of the armies taking part. These were distinguished by two characteristics in particular. In the first place, they were organizations designed to deliver, on the battlefield, the greatest possible concentration of *fire*. Cavalry was now almost an ancillary, if still an indispensable arm. Infantry won battles by its disciplined fire power, increasingly helped by artillery, which of course remained the primary arm in siege warfare. The need for a constant supply of ammunition would thus have tied armies to their supply lines even if they had been self-sufficient in food and in fodder for their horses; and although armies could requisition sufficient supplies from the countryside so long as they kept on the move, as soon as they were halted for any length of time they were driven back on their own resources. There was anyhow little disposition on the part of their officers to let troops forage for themselves. Consisting as they did of conscripted peasants or press-ganged 'volunteers', they were likely to use such liberty to desert altogether.

The movement of armies was thus tied to the small number of roads capable of carrying the huge convoys of their supply wagons, and most of those roads were guarded by fortresses that had to be besieged and reduced before further advance was possible. The need for fodder for draught animals and cavalry virtually constricted campaigning to the six months from May to October. In battle the need to develop maximum fire power produced linear tactics – the deployment of troops in long, thin lines blazing away at each other at point-blank range – which turned battles into murderous set-pieces that commanders of expensive regular forces avoided if they possibly could. It is not surprising that the ideal campaign should have been seen by military theorists as a war of manœuvre, preferably conducted on the territory of the enemy, in which one lived off the resources of his countryside and gradually wore him down.

This was the doctrine that Clausewitz set himself to demolish. One of his earliest published works was a critique of the contemporary theorist Heinrich von Bülow, who had in his works *Der Geist des neuren Kriegssystem* (The Spirit of the New System of War, 1799) and *Reine und angewandete Strategie* (Pure and Applied Strategy, 1804) elaborated a strategic doctrine based entirely on the requirements of the supply system and troop movements resulting from them. Bülow actually defined strategy as 'the science of military movements beyond the range of cannon-shot of either side'; as opposed to tactics, which was 'the science of military movements in the presence of the enemy'. Skilful strategy, maintained Bülow, reduced the need for tactical skills and might eliminate battle altogether. This the young Clausewitz dismissed as absurd. 'Strategy is *nothing* without fighting,' he wrote, 'for fighting is the material it uses, the means it employs.' The object of war, as of all creative activity, was 'the employment of the available means for the predetermined end'. Strategy Clausewitz therefore defined as 'the linking together (*Verbindung*) of separate battle engagements into a single whole, for the final object of the war'. Already at the age of 25 Clausewitz had laid down two principles of which his predecessors had lost sight. Military manœuvre was pointless unless it was designed to culminate in battle; and battle was pointless unless it was designed to serve the ultimate purpose of the war.

The political background

What the ultimate purpose of any campaign should *be* was a *political* question: a point that Clausewitz made in his first recorded reflections on strategy, written in 1804. Here, in a direct and uncomplicated fashion that contrasted starkly with the refined subtleties of his later writings, Clausewitz wrote simply 'The political object of war can be of two kinds; either to totally destroy the adversary, to eliminate his existence as a State, or else to prescribe peace terms to him.'

When he wrote these words Clausewitz had yet to experience the full fury of the campaign by which, two years later, Napoleon did come close to eliminating Prussia's existence as a State. But he had already lived through twelve years during which the whole tempo of warfare had been transformed; first by the French revolutionary armies that had overrun the Low Countries and threatened the Rhine between 1792 and 1795, then by Bonaparte's two lightning campaigns in Italy, in 1796–7 and 1799 – campaigns waged with an energy and for objectives far surpassing the limited means and petty purposes of warfare in earlier decades. As we have seen, it was not Clausewitz but his mentor Scharnhorst who first discerned how much of their military successes the French owed to their political transformation. As early as 1797, in an analysis of the causes of French successes and Allied failures, Scharnhorst had written that 'the succession of misfortunes that the Allied forces have encountered in the French revolutionary wars are closely interwoven with their domestic conditions, and those of the French nation'. The French armies were able successfully to break all the military rules because the politicians discarded all the normal political and economic constraints. For manpower they depended not on highly trained and expensive regular troops but on patriotic volunteers and, later, conscripts in apparently unlimited quantities whose services were virtually free. The French troops foraged for themselves, and if they deserted there were plenty more to take their place. Insufficiently trained for linear tactics in battle, they substituted a combination of free-firing skirmishers and dense columns of attack: first to wear down and then to overwhelm a defence that was in any case likely to be badly outnumbered. And to these hordes of self-sacrificing infantry Bonaparte was to add artillery in ever increasing proportions, and cavalry trained in merciless pursuit.

This was the terrible instrument with which Napoleon conquered Europe, but it was one available only to a government that was prepared to pour out men and money without stint, supported by a people who identified themselves with its objectives and submitted uncomplainingly to the sacrifices it demanded. There had in fact to be a nation; and was it possible to create a nation except, as the French had done, by the overthrow of monarchical institutions and the creation of a plebiscitary dictatorship ruling by terror? If not, the remedy was worse than the disease.

This was the problem that haunted Clausewitz throughout his active career, and it was as much a personal and moral as an abstract one. In 1806 the question which he had debated in the abstract at the Militärische Gesellschaft became a terrible reality. The catastrophe of Jena revealed not only that the Prussian Army was no match for the French, but that the people ruled by the Hohenzollern monarchy regarded the whole affair as no concern of theirs and observed the defeat of the royal troops with indifference. In internment in France, Clausewitz brooded on the contemptible lethargy of his own people. 'With whips would I stir the lazy animal', he wrote to his betrothed, 'and teach it to burst the chains with which out of cowardice and fear it permitted itself to be bound. I would spread an attitude throughout Germany which like an antidote would eliminate with destructive force the plague that is threatening to decay the spirit of the nation.' The problem that faced Prussia was one not just of military or even of political reform but one of moral renewal.

But was such moral renewal compatible with the retention of the old absolute monarchy, and of a dynasty that regarded all such liberal ideals with deep suspicion? For his part Clausewitz never doubted it: his loyalty to the dynasty remained unshakeable. But the dynasty, as we have seen, doubted him, and those who thought like him. The solution to which he and his colleagues looked forward, for the dynasty to set itself at the head of popular nationalist sentiment and to be carried onward instead of being swept aside by them, was achieved briefly between 1813 and 1815. But thereafter popular and monarchical sentiments again diverged and a regime was reimposed more repressive of nationalist sentiment than ever before. The political problem in Germany remained unsolved, and so did the military.

If the Revolutionary Wars could be regarded as a unique phenomenon, this did not greatly matter, but no one in his senses could believe that they were anything of the kind. Clausewitz certainly did not.

> War [*he wrote, probably towards the end of the 1820s*], untrammelled by any conventional restraints, had broken loose in all its elemental fury. This was due to the people's new share in these great affairs of state; and their participation, in turn, resulted partly from the impact that the Revolution had on the internal conditions of every state and partly from the danger that France posed to everyone.

> Will this always be the case in the future? From now on will every war in Europe be waged with the full resources of the State, and therefore have to be fought only over major issues that affect the people? Or shall we again see a gradual separation taking place between government and people? Such questions are difficult to answer, and we are the last to dare to do so. But the reader will agree with us when we say that *once barriers – which in a sense consist only in man's ignorance of the possible – are torn down, they are not easily set up again.* At least when major interests are at stake, mutual hostility will express itself in the same manner as it has in our own day. (p. 593; emphasis added)

Napoleonic warfare, Clausewitz discerned, was thus more likely than not to be the model for the future, and armies unready to fight it would once again be destroyed as completely as the Austrians had been at Austerlitz and the Prussians at Jena. And if a political transformation was needed to make successful participation in such a war possible, this was a price that any self-respecting people, he indicated, must be prepared to pay.

The writing of *On War*

When he accepted the Directorship of the War College in 1818 Clausewitz was still only 38 years old, but he had behind him twenty-five years of experience, as extensive as it was varied, and he had at his disposal hundreds of pages of his own writings on every aspect of war. He had already begun to put these together in the hope that he could distil from them some fairly pithy observations about strategy intended for the expert reader. But, as he confessed,

> my nature, which always drives me to develop and systematize, eventually asserted itself. The more I wrote and surrendered to the spirit of analysis, the more I reverted to a more systematic approach, and so one chapter after another was added. In the end I intended to revise it all again, strengthen the causal connections in the earlier essays, perhaps in the later ones draw together several analyses into a single conclusion, and thus produce a reasonable whole . . . (p. 63)

He never did so. Twelve years later, on leaving the college, he wrote 'the manuscript on the conduct of major operations that will be found after my death can in its present state be regarded as nothing but a collection of materials from which a theory of war *was to have been distilled*' (p. 70; emphasis added). The twelve years had been taken up with revising, redrafting, and the collection of new material, including the writing of original studies of most of the Napoleonic campaigns. In about 1827, when he had drafted six of his projected eight books, he thought he had found the connecting thread that would bind all his ideas together. It was not any new idea. He had expounded it in his first essay nearly a quarter of a century earlier, when he emphasized the primacy of policy in determining the object of the war and explained the double nature of war, as potentially both limited and total, that resulted from this.

Determined to make this the main theme of this work Clausewitz began to redraft the whole work again, and completed the first chapter to his satisfaction. But even as he redrafted yet another idea came to him: that of war as a 'remarkable trinity', in which the directing policy of the government, the professional qualities of the army, and the attitude of the population all played an equally significant part. His mind was so fertile in ideas and analogies, his quest for precision so exacting that, even if he had been able to complete his revision, it is unlikely that he would ever have been satisfied with it. However long he lived he would probably have bequeathed to posterity only 'a collection of materials from which a theory of war was to have been distilled'. But he could still with reason claim that

> an unprejudiced reader in search of truth and understanding will recognise the fact that [the contents] for all their imperfection of form, contain the fruit of years of reflection on war and diligent study of it. He may even find they contain the basic ideas that might bring about a revolution in the theory of war. (p. 70)

It is these ideas that we shall examine in the following pages.

Chapter 2
Theory and practice in war

The first problem Clausewitz had to solve was this: how was it possible to have a 'theory' of war at all? It was not simply a matter of combating the crude pragmatism to which all soldiers are temperamentally prone, the belief that theorizing is a lot of nonsense and that all military problems which are not purely technical ones can be solved by a mixture of courage and common sense. With this attitude indeed Clausewitz had a great deal of sympathy, and his writing was, as we shall see, to provide some justification for it. More important was the task of explaining why all theories advanced in the past, and indeed in his own day, had been so inadequate if not indeed positively misleading, and how in spite of this gloomy record it might still be possible to be right.

Apart from the authors of memoirs and narrative histories, writers on war had hitherto fallen into three categories. The great majority had dealt with purely practical questions of armament, supply, drill, and deployment – matters which, in Clausewitz's words, bore the same relationship to the art of generalship as the craft of the swordsmith did to the art of fencing. It was indeed the narrow concentration on these minutiae, which he had no doubt observed in so many senior officers in the Prussian Army, that he was most anxious to avoid.

> Military activity in general [*he wrote*] is served by an enormous amount of expertise and skills, all of which are needed to place a well-equipped

force in the field. They coalesce into a few great results before they attain their final purpose in war, like streams combining to form rivers before they flow into the sea. The man who wishes to control them must familiarize himself only with those activities that empty themselves into the great oceans of war ... Only this explains why in war men have so often successfully emerged in the higher ranks, and even as supreme commanders, whose former field of endeavour was entirely different; the fact, indeed, that distinguished commanders have never emerged from the ranks of the most erudite or scholarly officers, but have been for *the* most part men whose station in life could not have brought them a high degree of education. (p. 144)

For these 'learned' officers, *Gelehrte, Pedanten*, as he dismissively described them, Clausewitz had nothing but contempt. They were necessary drudges, to be kept firmly in their subordinate places. The trouble was, however, that the obvious irrelevance of their expertise to the real art of command had led to the opposite fallacy which characterized the second category of writers; those antinomians who 'rejected all belief in theory and postulated that war was a natural function of man which he performed as well as his aptitude permitted' (p. 145). There could be no 'principles of war', according to this school of thought; everything was a matter of individual genius that could be neither imitated nor analysed. The appearance of a Frederick or of a Bonaparte was as unpredictable as that of a Shakespeare or a Mozart; they were exceptional, paranormal phenomena, and to seek for the secret of their success was a waste of time. (The most striking statement of this view is to be found in Georg von Berenhorst, *Betrachtungen über die Kriegskunst*, 1797.)

Clausewitz had some sympathy with this view, describing it merely as 'overstated'. He reserved his fire for the third and more numerous school; those writers who did believe it possible to study war as a science and to lay down immutable principles for its conduct. This may have been feasible, he allowed, within the limited field of siegecraft, in which so many factors were quantifiable – the range and destructive power of guns, mathematically calculable lines of sight and angles of fire, the supplies required for garrisons of determinate sizes, the time taken to dig and complete trenches. But Lloyd and his successors had tried, as we have seen, to extend this kind of precision to the whole conduct of war, and their ideas had in consequence, thought Clausewitz, been grossly misleading.

Probably the most extreme, though certainly not the most respected of such writers was Heinrich von Bülow, whose work we have already met. His belief in the primacy of the supply factor led him to postulate that the secret of successful operations lay in ensuring that the angle formed at the objective by lines drawn from the extreme ends of the base line from which the army was operating should be not less than $90°$, an assumption on which he went on to base a whole range of abstruse calculations. A more formidable exponent of such views was Antoine de Jomini, Clausewitz's contemporary and rival, a military analyst whose depth, scope, and readability made him the most influential writer on military affairs outside Germany until the end of the nineteenth century. Jomini believed that there was a common formula underlying the successes of both Napoleon and Frederick the Great that could be summarized as 'directing the mass of one's forces successively on the decisive points in the theatre of war, and as far as possible against the communications of the enemy without disrupting one's own': an object that could best be achieved by the mastery of what he termed (as everyone else has ever since) 'interior lines'.

Clausewitz denied the validity of such formulations, not so much because they were oversimplifications, but because they ignored what he saw as the essence of war.

They aim at fixed values; but in war everything is uncertain, and calculations have to be made with variable quantities.

They direct the inquiry exclusively towards physical quantities, whereas all military action is intertwined with psychological forces and effects. They consider only unilateral action, whereas war consists of a continuous interaction of opposites. (p. 136)

No theory could be of any value, he maintained, that did not take account of these interconnected elements – the uncertainty of all information, the importance of moral factors, and, lending emphasis to both of these, the unpredictable reactions of the adversary. The element of uncertainty arose very largely from the impossibility of gauging enemy intentions and reactions, something that was particularly difficult when there were no overmastering political incentives to determine his military decisions. At best one could only work on probabilities, and in doing this, however good one's judgement, there would always be a substantial element of sheer luck. Even the best generals were successful gamblers who had the nerve to back their judgement. No amount of theory could, in a moment of crisis, tell them what to do.

This was one reason, in Clausewitz's view, why moral forces were so important. 'With uncertainty in one scale, courage and self-confidence must be thrown into the other to correct the balance.' But there was another, far more fundamental reason, and one that all theorists had ignored. War was *dangerous*; so dangerous that no one who had not taken part in it could conceive what it was like; how in war 'the light of reason' as he put it in a piece of classic understatement 'is refracted in a manner quite different from what is normal in academic speculation' (p. 113). If war was the realm of uncertainty and chance, even more was it the realm of suffering, confusion, exhaustion, and fear. All these factors combined to create the element that Clausewitz termed *friction*: the environment in which all military action took place (pp. 119–21).

Everything in war is very simple, but the simplest thing is very diffi-cult ... Countless minor incidents – the kind you can never really

25

foresee – combine to lower the general level of performance, so that one always falls far short of the intended goal . . . The military machine . . . is basically very simple and very easy to manage. But we should bear in mind that none of its components is of one piece: each part is composed of individuals, every one of whom retains his potential of friction . . . A battalion is made up of individuals, the least important of whom may chance to delay things and sometimes make them go wrong.

This inherent tendency for things to go wrong (one widely known and feared in all armies and known in the British Army as 'Murphy's Law') was compounded by external and even less controllable factors, such as the weather.

Fog can prevent the enemy from being seen in time, a gun from firing when it should, a report from reaching the commanding officer. Rain can prevent a battalion from arriving, make another late by keeping it not three but eight hours on the march, ruin a cavalry charge by bogging the horses down in mud, etc.

In short,

Action in war is like movement in a resistant element. Just as the simplest and most natural of movements, walking, cannot easily be performed in water, so in war, it is difficult for normal efforts to achieve even moderate results.

It was this friction, said Clausewitz, that 'distinguishes real war from war on paper', and an understanding of its importance had to be the starting-point for any theorist. A commander in the field could seldom be sure exactly where the enemy was or in what strength, much less what he was likely to do. Sometimes he did not know the location and condition even of his own troops. He, and even more the men under his command, was likely to be tired, hungry, and apprehensive if not actually physically frightened. Under these circumstances what mattered was not the logistical calculations of staff officers; it was the vital but incalculable factor of *morale*. In the last analysis it was at moral not physical strength that all military action was directed: 'All war assumes human weakness and seeks to exploit it' (p. 185). Or, as he also put it, 'war is a trial of moral and physical forces by means of the latter'. 'One might say that the physical seem little more than the wooden hilt, while the moral factors are the precious metal, the real weapon, the finely-honed blade.'

The first of the eight books that make up *On War* is therefore very largely devoted to the question of 'moral forces': those of the commander, those of the army, and those (less fully considered) of the people. About the importance of the latter Clausewitz was fully aware and he had written prolifically about the subject in the course of his career. In *On War* he did not ignore it: he dealt with the relationship of military professionalism and popular support, with what could reasonably be expected of volunteer forces and what could not. But in the actual conduct of operations the essential factors were bound to be the talents of the general and the quality of the troops under his command, and it was these that Clausewitz treated most extensively.

The qualities of the commander Clausewitz covered in a chapter entitled 'On Military Genius', a much used and abused term of his time which he tried to strip of the myths that had accumulated around it. For him 'genius' was not something paranormal or God-given but simply 'a very highly developed mental aptitude for a particular occupation'. Military genius, like any other, consisted in 'a harmonious combination of elements, in which one or the other ability may predominate but none may be in conflict with the rest' (p. 100). These elements included high intelligence (only advanced civilizations, he maintained, could produce really great soldiers), and courage both physical and moral. But there were two qualities derivative from these on which Clausewitz laid particular stress. The first was intuitive, the quality labelled by the French *coup d'œil*: the almost instinctive capacity to discern through the fog of war what was happening and what needed to be done; a flair for essentials that enabled the commander to select the right course almost without thinking, and certainly without going through the elaborate process of calculations of possibilities and probabilities that would paralyse the decisions of a lesser man.

The second requisite, said Clausewitz, was the capacity, having taken a decision, to stick to it: *determination*. Everything would conspire to convince the general that his decision had been wrong: conflicting intelligence or, worse, the absence of any intelligence at all; the doubts of his subordinates; and the gradual exhaustion of the forces under his command, the decline in whose moral strength had to be made up for by the greater exertion of his own.

> So long as a unit fights cheerfully, with spirit and élan, great strength of will is rarely needed; but once conditions become difficult, as they must when much is at stake, things no longer run like a well-oiled machine. The machine itself begins to resist, and the commander needs tremendous will-power to overcome this resistance. As each man's strength gives out, as it no longer responds to his will, the inertia of the whole gradually comes to rest on the commander's will alone. (p. 104)

The quality of determination was different from mere obstinacy. It was rooted in intellectual insight and composed of a rare blend of intellect and moral courage. The whole question of the relationship between determination, firmness, obstinacy, and strength of mind, between those familiar opposites of 'character' and 'intellect' that were to cause so much pedagogical debate and still sometimes do, was discussed by Clausewitz with a shrewdness and a precision that gives to these pages an intrinsic value far transcending their military context.

The moral qualities demanded of the troops Clausewitz discussed elsewhere, in a chapter entitled 'Military Virtues of an Army'. In this he distinguished the spirit that animated professional troops from the qualities – bravery, adaptability, stamina, enthusiasm – that inspired a people in arms.

> No matter how clearly we see the citizen and the soldier in the same man, how strongly we conceive of war as the business of the entire nation . . . the business of war will always be individual and distinct. Consequently, for as long as they practise this activity, soldiers will think of themselves as members of a kind of guild, in whose regulations, laws and customs the spirit of war is given pride of place. (p. 187)

At the heart of any army, there would always be a cadre of professionals who would fight, not out of patriotism but, as had the forces of the eighteenth century, from sheer professional pride. Of the virtues of such professionals Clausewitz wrote with unreserved admiration:

> An army that maintains its cohesion under the most murderous fire; that cannot be shaken by imaginary fears and resists well-found ones with all its might; that, proud of its victories, will not lose the strength to obey orders and its respect and trust for its officers even in defeat; whose physical power, like the muscles of an athlete, has been steeled by training in privation and effort; . . . that is mindful of all these duties and qualities by virtue of the single powerful idea of the honour of its arms – such an army is imbued with the true military spirit. (p. 187)

This military spirit, said Clausewitz, stood 'in the same relationship to the parts of an army as does a general's ability to the whole'. The general could give only overall direction. 'At the point where the separate parts need guidance, the military spirit must take command' (p. 188). And if this spirit was for any reason not in evidence it had to be made up for by some other means, by the superior ability of the general or the 'martial virtues' of the people. It was a quality that could be created only by frequent wars or very severe training, and even then appearances could be deceptive, as Clausewitz knew only too well after his observation of the fate that overtook the Prussian Army in 1806.

One should be careful not to compare this expanded and refined solidarity of a brotherhood of tempered, battle-scarred veterans with the self-esteem and vanity of regular armies which are patched together by service regulations and drill. Grim severity and iron discipline may be able to preserve the military virtues of a unit, but it cannot create them ... An army like this will be able to prevail only by virtue of its commander, never on its own. (p. 189)

Moral factors, then, were the ultimate determinants in war, and no theory could be valid that did not give them their full value. But how did they interact with the physical factors – all those mundane questions of logistics, weapon capabilities, topography, and tactics on which earlier military writers had concentrated so exclusively? How indeed could one theorize about such intangible qualities at all? This was a problem, Clausewitz pointed out, that was not peculiar to the military. It was common to many activities, particularly in the realm of the arts. There one found very much the same kind of interaction between the material and the intangible. The painter, or the sculptor, or the architect, used matter as the means of expressing intangible, unquantifiable qualities of the spirit. His materials might constrain that expression but, in the hands of a master at least, they did not dictate it. In aesthetics theorists did not make rules which ordinary men had to obey but geniuses were somehow able to transcend. On the contrary, theorists studied, analysed, and within limits explained what those geniuses had done. It was indeed the activity of the geniuses, of the masters of their craft, that *made* the rules.

So it was with war. One could only learn how to conduct war, said Clausewitz, by learning, and learning *from*, what had already been done; by studying war not in the abstract but in the reality. Only thus could a truly comprehensive theory of war be developed, one that would make it possible not only to understand (as with painting or architecture) what the great masters had achieved, but to appreciate how their achievements came to be creative and not imitative acts, unique in themselves but enlarging the scope of expression available to their successors.

This meant studying the history of war, for 'in the art of war experience counts for more than any number of abstract truths' (p. 164). But the study of that history had itself to be an exercise of critical judgement. One could not take for granted the reliability of historians. The bulk of histories, Clausewitz warned, were indeed so unreliable as to be almost useless. Most of what had come down from antiquity or the Middle Ages was too incomplete and inaccurate to be of value, even when it was not pure myth. Clausewitz was prepared to accept as material for study only those campaigns about which full and accurate knowledge was obtainable, which effectively restricted him to those fought in Europe, and predominantly Western Europe, during the past two centuries.

This historical data had to be subjected to three distinct processes. First there was historical research proper – the winnowing of fact from rumour, hypothesis and fiction; the establishment of a reliable record (as his younger contemporary Leopold von Ranke was to put it, *wie es eigentlich gewesen*) of events as they actually occurred. For the serious military historian this presented sometimes quite intractable problems, but their solution had always to be his first priority. Secondly came the complex process of relating cause to effect; having expounded *what* happened, to go on to explain *why*. Only then was it possible to go on to the application of critical judgement, the evaluation of the means employed by the commanders concerned, the assessment of their successes and failures. But such judgement was not possible unless one had already developed some kind of a theory, some concept of what, under given circumstances, was the most appropriate action for the general to take. The formulation of a theory and its application was indeed a continuous and reciprocal activity, historical knowledge moulding theory, theory illuminating historical judgement. But, insisted Clausewitz, 'The function of criticism would be missed entirely if criticism were to degenerate into a mechanical application of theory . . .

31

A critic should never use the results of theory as laws or standards but only – as the soldier does – as aids to judgement' (p. 157).

If the critic had to be cautious in his application of theory, so also had the soldier. He could not expect the theorist to provide all the answers to his problems, 'stamping out war plans as from a kind of truth-machine' (p. 168). At the highest levels of command, Clausewitz admitted, theory could furnish only very limited help. The uncertainties were too great, the range of possibilities too vast, the array of factors to be taken into account far too diverse. It was here that the *coup d'œil* of the great commander was needed to enable him to analyse the situation and find his own solutions for himself. Precedent was unlikely to be a reliable guide; he had to create his own precedents. But the further one descended the hierarchy of command, the more limited the range of factors became and the less scope there was for the intrusion of the contingent, the unpredictable; until at the level of minor tactics it really did become possible to prescribe specific routines to deal with specific situations, to produce manuals and drills which, if scrupulously followed by obedient and unimaginative subordinates, had a very high probability of success. Such prescription was necessary in any case, since the chances of finding at the lower levels of command sufficient officers on whose powers of judgement and *coup d'œil* one could entirely rely were slim indeed. Most of them had to be told exactly what to do, and be able to give instantaneous stock responses to the limited range of situations likely to confront them in their narrow range of command. To the great mass of troops, indeed, theory filtered down only as drill. It became, on the battlefield, a necessary substitute for thought.

But even at the highest levels, Clausewitz insisted, the theorist could make a significant contribution so long as he realized his limitations. His role was to *educate the judgement* of the commander; not to tell him what to do. At the very least, theory should help him get his ideas in order:

32

Theory exists so that one does not have to start afresh every time sorting out the raw material and ploughing through it, but will find it ready to hand and in good order. It is meant to educate the mind of the future commander, or, more accurately, to guide him in his self-education; not accompany him to the battlefield. (p. 141)

Here we can see the influence of Clausewitz's early studies in educational theory. The wise teacher, he had then learned, regarded his subject-matter not as an end in itself but as a means to an end, which was the development of the potentialities of his pupil to the full. The theorist might lay down guiding principles, if indeed his studies resulted in the emergence of such principles (and as to whether they would or should Clausewitz remained agnostic; certainly he himself laid down no 'principles of war'); but no principles or roles would be of any value unless they had been thoroughly assimilated. The commander had to obey principles as the product of his own judgement, not of someone else's, and certainly not as a kind of objective scientific 'law'. Indeed, the more a theory proceeded 'from the objective form of a science to the subjective form of a skill', argued Clausewitz, the more effective it would prove (p. 141). It was not a matter of *wissen*, 'knowing that', but of *können*, 'knowing how'.

Did this mean that war was an art rather than a science? Clausewitz had no doubt on the subject. 'The term "science"', he declared, 'should be kept for disciplines such as mathematics and astronomy, whose object is pure knowledge' (p. 148). But the dichotomy was a misleading one. All arts involved the application of some scientific knowledge; all sciences involved the utilization of judgement; which implies art, and in any case war did not belong in these categories at all. It was, argued Clausewitz, a social activity, part of man's social existence:

War is a clash between major interests that is resolved by bloodshed – that is the only way in which it differs from other conflicts. Rather than

33

comparing it to an art we could more accurately compare it to commerce, which is also a conflict of human interests and activities; and it is still closer to politics, which in turn may be considered as a kind of commerce on a larger scale. (p. 149)

Any theory of war was thus a branch of social and political theory and had to be considered in the context of politics, 'the womb in which war develops – where its outlines already exist in their hidden, rudimentary form, like the characteristics of living creatures in their embryos'.

Clausewitz's teaching about the relationship of politics and war I shall consider further in the next chapter. Here I may fittingly conclude with his summary of the contribution that he believed the theorist could make to the practical conduct of war.

Theory will have fulfilled its main task when it is used to analyse the constituent elements of war, to distinguish precisely what at first sight seems fused, to explain in full the properties of the means employed and to show their probable effects, to define clearly the nature of the ends in view and to illuminate all phases of warfare in a thorough critical enquiry. Theory then becomes a guide to anyone who wants to learn about war from books; it will light his way, ease his progress, train his judgement, and help him avoid pitfalls. (p. 141)

But it could never tell him exactly what to do.

Chapter 3
Ends and means in war

Clausewitz thus justified the utility of theorizing about war so long as the theorist knew his limitations, and so long as he gave full weight to the unquantifiable moral factors involved as well as the quantifiable physical ones. The interaction between these elements, the moral and the physical, was indeed the basis of his whole theoretical approach. War for him was a constant dialectic between them, each penetrating and acting upon the other.

This model of a dialectic between opposed but linked concepts clearly fascinated Clausewitz, as it did so many of his contemporaries among German thinkers. The treatment of the relationship between physical and moral forces is one example of this. That between historical knowledge and critical judgement, which we have also touched on, was another. So was that, familiar in his time, between the 'Idea' and its manifestations, between 'absolute' and 'real' war. So was the dialectic between attack and defence; and so, most important of all, was that between ends and means. The dialectic was not Hegelian: it led to no synthesis which itself conjured up its antithesis. Rather it was a continuous interaction between opposite poles, each fully comprehensible only in terms of the other. One could not understand the *nature* of war unless one appreciated the dialectic between moral and physical forces. But one could not have a practical theory for the *conduct* of war unless one understood the relationship between ends and means; in particular the political end of war and the military means used to attain it.

It was only in the last years of his life that Clausewitz came to his famous conclusion that 'war was *nothing* but the continuation of policy with other means' or, more explicitly, '*simply* the continuation of policy with the admixture of other means' (pp. 69, 605; emphasis added). But we have already seen how in his very earliest writings in 1804–5 he referred to the political object of war, without any indication that he was saying anything original or controversial. The idea was probably a commonplace at the time among Scharnhorst's circle. At the same period Clausewitz put forward, equally as a commonplace, the theory of the two types of war; of war 'either to totally destroy the enemy . . . or else to prescribe peace terms to him'. He laid far more stress on the significance, not only of war itself, but of operations within war as means to specific ends, to be evaluated in terms of their effectiveness as such. It was for this, among other reasons, that he took Bülow to task. Bülow's definition of strategy and tactics in terms of marches beyond or within the range of the enemy was, maintained Clausewitz, 'unphilosophical to the highest degree', because it missed the whole point. The object of any art, he insisted, was 'the employment of the available means (*Mittel*) for the predetermined end (*Zweck*)'. His own definition was quite clear: 'tactics was the doctrine of the use of armed forces in battle, strategy the doctrine of the use of individual battles for the purpose of the war'.

This duality of means and ends, *Mittel* and *Zweck*, runs throughout Clausewitz's entire work. He drew however a further distinction: that between the *final purpose* of the war, and the *intermediate stages* by which it was reached. The latter were the objectives (*Ziele*) of the subordinate military commanders; but they were the means by which the strategist attained his own final object, his *Zweck*. No military success could be judged in isolation, for it was itself only one stage in the strategist's overall plan. The *objectives* assigned to subordinate units – the capture of a bridge or a fortress, the occupation of a province, the destruction of an enemy force – were the *means* by which the general achieved his own higher purposes; and ultimately those purposes were not military at all but political, 'the ends that lead directly to peace' (p. 143).

Political requirements might present a wide array of objects for the strategist to attain, but there was only one means of attaining them, insisted Clausewitz: *fighting*. That was where Bülow had gone wrong. The instruments at the commander's disposal, the physical elements through which he exercised his creative talent, were not the armed forces themselves, much less their movements. It was their fighting activity. 'The end for which a soldier is recruited, clothed, armed and trained', Clausewitz reminded us, 'the whole object of his sleeping, eating, drinking and marching is simply that he should fight at the right place and the right time' (p. 95). He had no other purpose: the whole apparatus of maintenance and supply which had dominated the thinking of so many military writers existed simply to make fighting possible; obvious enough when one states it, but something that many strategic theorists tended, and still occasionally tend, to forget.

For this activity of fighting Clausewitz sometimes used the word *der Kampf*, but more often, and somewhat confusingly, *das Gefecht*. The trouble with *das Gefecht* is that it can mean two distinct things. It can mean the activity of fighting in general; but it can also indicate a specific kind of a fight, one limited in time and scope, which in British military parlance is usually called by the anodyne term 'the engagement'. A more exact translation is available in American English in the word 'combat', which expresses exactly the ambiguity of the original, as an activity either general or specific. But that ambiguity is confusing for our purposes, and the word 'engagement' expresses very well that precise and distinct confrontation of forces which Clausewitz normally meant by the term; a confrontation limited *in scope* by the capacity of a single individual to control it, and *in time* by the resolution of the issue over

37

which the engagement was fought – the attainment, or abandonment, of its objective (*Ziel*).

These engagements Clausewitz saw as the constituent elements out of which strategy was constructed, the building blocks that made up the totality of the war. They were both ends and means. They were *ends* in that forces were raised, maintained, and deployed in the field in order to fight them. They were *means* in that their results were springboards for the attainment of yet further ends. This was the true relationship between tactics and strategy. Tactics was concerned with engagements, their planning and execution; strategy was the coordination of these engagements to attain the object of the war. 'In tactics', wrote Clausewitz, 'the means are fighting forces trained for combat; the end is victory.' For the strategist victorious engagements were his means; his ends were 'those objects which lead directly to peace' (pp. 142–3). The most splendid of victories was thus nothing in itself unless it was also the means to the attainment of a political end; whether that end was the total destruction of the enemy state or the laying down of whatever peace terms policy might require.

At the highest levels therefore there could be no distinction drawn between strategy and statesmanship, and the strategist's achievements had ultimately to be judged not in military but in political terms. But the criterion of his performance was the same as any other art; how effectively he had used the means at his disposal to achieve his desired end. 'A prince or a general', wrote Clausewitz, 'can best show his genius by managing a campaign exactly to suit his resources, doing neither too much or too little' (p. 177). By these standards he was able to applaud both of those very different masters of their craft, Bonaparte and Frederick the Great. The unlimited aims of the former could have been pursued only by the ruthless application of the unlimited means at his disposal. His political object might be condemned, but his method of achieving it could not. As for Frederick, with his limited object of

38

retaining his Silesian conquests of 1741, his military performance had been masterly; not because of the elegance of his marches and manœuvres, but because in pursuing *a* major objective with limited resources, 'he did not try to undertake anything beyond his strength, but always just enough to get him what he wanted'. 'His whole conduct of war . . . shows an element of restrained strength, which was always in balance, never lacking in vigour, rising to remarkable heights in moments of crisis, but immediately afterwards reverting to a state of calm oscillation, always ready to adjust to the smallest shift in the political situation' (p. 179).

The example of Frederick the Great and of Bonaparte suggested that wars should ideally be fought by princes who combined in their own persons political and military leadership and who could be oblivious to public opinion. This obviously was too much to hope for in the generality of cases, and the direction of war was likely to be a more cumbrous process, as it had been in the Prussia of Clausewitz's own day. But, however matters were managed, Clausewitz insisted, the political leadership had to have the last word. Political leaders were not indeed infallible, but

> Only if statesmen look to certain military moves and actions to produce effects that are foreign to their nature do political decisions influence operations for the worse. In the same way as a man who has not fully mastered a foreign language sometimes fails to express himself correctly, so statesmen often issue orders that defeat the purpose they are meant to serve. (p. 608)

To prevent this from happening the political leadership needed both to possess a good general grasp of military policy and to be in constant consultation with the military command. This was best achieved, wrote Clausewitz, in two ways: first, 'by making the commander-in-chief a member of the cabinet, so that the cabinet can share in the major aspects (*Hauptmomenten*) of his activities'; and secondly, by the cabinet establishing itself in the theatre of war, as the Prussian cabinet had in 1813–15. Clausewitz's editors, when a second edition of *On War* was published in 1853, altered the sentence quoted to read 'so that he (the commander-in-chief) may take part in its councils and decisions on important occasions'. Some scholars have seen in this a deliberate distortion of Clausewitz's meaning so as to give the military a greater say in decision-making than he had intended. But it can equally be seen as a misguided attempt to provide clarification of a passage which, with good reason, might be considered somewhat obscure.

The nature of policy determined the nature of the war, and political circumstances accordingly shaped strategy. Clausewitz explained how this happened – or, at least, how according to his theory it *ought* to happen. 'What the theorist has to say here is this: one must keep the dominant characteristics of both belligerents in mind. Out of those characteristics a certain centre of gravity develops, the hub of all power and movement, on which everything depends. That is the point at which all our energies should be directed' (p. 595). Clausewitz cited three examples of such 'centres of gravity': the opponent's army, his capital, and, if he had a stronger protector, the army of his ally. Since all of these were vulnerable to attack, said Clausewitz, 'the defeat and destruction of his fighting force remains the best way to begin, and will in any case be a very significant feature of the campaign' (p. 596). Political considerations might however compel the modification or the postponement of this objective. In that case, he admitted, 'we must also be willing to wage minimal wars, which consist in merely threatening the enemy, with negotiations held in reserve' (p. 604): a situation we shall consider when we come to Clausewitz's doctrine of 'limited war'. But Clausewitz made it clear that he regarded this type of campaign as less than satisfactory. The ideal strategy, he indicated, was to identify the enemy's centre of gravity and then to direct all one's energies against it; and if the centre of gravity proved to be the opposing army, so much the better.

If the enemy is thrown off balance, he must not be given time to recover. Blow after blow must be struck in the same direction; the victor, in other words, must strike with all his strength, and not just against a fraction of the enemy's. Not by taking things the easy way – using superior strength to filch some province, preferring the security of the minor conquest to a major success – but by constantly seeking out his centre of power, by daring all to win all, will one really defeat the enemy. (p. 596)

It can be argued that this strategic doctrine was banal to the point of brutality. Perhaps we should not blame Clausewitz for having failed to consider the use of any but military means for achieving his strategic ends – the use of diplomacy rather than force to neutralize the enemy's allies, for example, or of propaganda and subversion to influence his public opinion. Such methods, he might have replied, were the business of the political leadership, not of the military commander. But we can certainly comment critically on the absence from his list of possible 'centres of gravity' of the enemy's economic capacity to carry on the war at all. This, after all, had been a primary objective in the almost continuous wars between Britain, Spain, the Netherlands, and France over the previous two hundred years – wars fought in a maritime dimension of which Clausewitz, for all his interest in military history, never showed the slightest awareness.

It is not easy, however, to give a fair and comprehensive summary of Clausewitz's strategic doctrine, since it is presented with infuriating incoherence. Key passages relating to it are scattered almost at random throughout *On War*, fully bearing out his gloomy prophecy that his readers would find in the book only 'a collection of material from which a theory of war was to have been distilled'. The section of the work entitled 'On Strategy in General' is only a collection of chapters on diverse topics linked by no very evident common theme. A casual reader might very reasonably assume that Clausewitz's interest in the overall problems of strategy was slight in comparison with his almost obsessive concern with what he saw as the main tool of the strategist – the engagement, and in particular the major battle; a topic to which he devoted an entire book, perhaps the most powerfully written and best organized in the whole of *On War*.

In presenting Clausewitz's strategic doctrine in its totality, we might begin with his oft-quoted and surely sardonic observation, 'The best strategy is always to be *very strong*; first in general, and then at the decisive point' (p. 204). The argument for this is more subtle than appears at first sight. Superior forces, Clausewitz pointed out, always provide the best chance of winning a battle. Obviously it is desirable that the skill of your commanders, the training of your troops, and the morale of your forces should surpass that of your adversary, but these are matters that do not necessarily lie within your control. It is always wisest to assume that in these qualities the two sides will be evenly matched. Even if they are not, there is a limit beyond which tactical skill and high morale cannot compensate for numerical inferiority, except in such special circumstances as the defence of mountain passes. Sooner or later numbers would always tell. So the larger the army the commander brought into the field, the better the chances he gave to his subordinate units of winning in their individual engagements.

If superiority of numbers was impossible, then, said Clausewitz, 'the forces available must be deployed with such skill that even in the absence of an absolute superiority, a relative superiority is attained at the decisive point' (p. 196). This was where the talents of the strategist were necessary; the *coup d'œil* to distinguish the decisive point and the resolution to concentrate everything available against it, stripping forces from secondary fronts and ignoring lesser objectives. This had been the secret of Bonaparte's success, but it did not take a Clausewitz to discern it. Jomini, as we have seen, made the same point in his own writings, and expounded it at far greater length – only to receive from Clausewitz the dismissive comment, 'to reduce the whole secret of the art of war to the formula of numerical superiority *at a certain time in a certain place* was an over-simplification that would not have stood up for a moment against the realities of life' (p. 135). Jomini's own formula does not at first look very different from Clausewitz's own – 'the best strategy is to be *very strong*; first in general, and then at the decisive point' (p. 204). But whereas Jomini spent many chapters in analysing where and what the decisive point might be, Clausewitz saw the main problem as the moral one; the capacity of the commander to maintain his determination, in spite of all temptations to the contrary, to concentrate his forces against that decisive point.

Clausewitz's discussion of strategy was indeed dominated, if not distorted, by his desire to disprove the idea, so current in the eighteenth century, that skilful strategic combinations could make tactical confrontation unnecessary, that the strategist might have any means to serve his purposes other than hard fighting.

> How are we to counter the highly sophisticated theory that supposes it possible for a particularly ingenious method of inflicting minor damage on the enemy's forces to lead to major indirect destruction; or that claims to produce, by means of limited but skilfully applied blows, such a paralysis of the enemy's forces and control of his will-power as to constitute a significant short cut to victory? Admittedly an engagement at one point may be worth more than at another. Admittedly there may be a skilful ordering of priority of engagements in strategy; indeed that is what strategy is all about, and we do not wish to deny it. We do claim, however, that direct annihilation of the enemy's forces must always be the *dominant consideration*. We simply want to establish this dominance of the destructive principle. (p. 223)

This casual reference to 'the ordering of priorities in strategy' and the admission 'that is what strategy is all about' is all he has to say about a matter to which other strategic writers – Jomini himself, and the English writer Edward Bruce Hamley (1824–93) – devoted entire works. But it must be read together with a passage from another section in *On War*: one that Clausewitz's editors considered to be an unfinished draft, but

43

is quite central to Clausewitz's strategic thought. Under the cumbrous heading 'Possible Engagements Are to be Regarded as Real Ones Because of their Consequences', Clausewitz explained further what he meant by this 'priority of engagements'. Engagements, he there pointed out, could achieve their objective *even if they were not fought.*

> If troops are sent to cut off a retreating enemy and he thereupon surrenders without further fight, his decision is caused solely by the threat of a fight posed by those troops. If part of our army occupies an undefended enemy province ... the factor making it possible for our force to hold the province is the engagement the enemy must expect to fight if he tries to retake it. In both cases results have been produced by the mere possibility of an engagement. The possibility has acquired reality. (p. 181)

Further, it might be necessary to fight a series of preliminary engagements in order to place oneself in such an advantageous position *vis-à-vis* the enemy's forces, by capturing roads, bridges, supply dumps, towns, or even whole provinces. These acquisitions, said Clausewitz, 'should always be regarded merely as a means of gaining greater superiority, *so that in the end we are able to offer an engagement to the enemy when he is in no position to accept it*' (emphasis added).

This might seem to present the very possibility that Clausewitz was so anxious to deny, that of bloodless victory through skilful manœuvre. But the victory could be bloodless only if the strategist was *prepared* to shed blood; to fight and win, at whatever cost, the engagements he offered to the enemy. 'All action is undertaken', as Clausewitz wrote in yet another section of *On War*, 'in the belief that if the ultimate test of arms should actually occur, the outcome would *be favourable*' (p. 97). And he went on to use an analogy that later was to tickle the fancy of Marx and Engels: 'The decision by arms is for all major and minor operations in war what cash payment is in commerce. No matter how complex the relationship between the two parties, no matter how rarely settlements occur, they can never be entirely absent.' In the same way, however ingenious the manoeuvres and combinations, however skilfully contrived the marches, none of them were of the slightest value unless at the end of it all the general was in a position to fight, and to win.

What happened in those 'cash settlements' was therefore more significant than the calculations and movements that led up to them. Every such settlement, wrote Clausewitz, was 'a bloody and destructive test of physical and moral strength. Whoever has the greater sum of both left at the end is the victor' (p. 231). It was because these tests were so decisive for the success of any strategy that Clausewitz devoted to them an entire book.

About the purpose of the engagement Clausewitz was very clear. It was the destruction (*Vernichtung*) of the enemy forces. There might be other objectives, such as those described above – the control of terrain, of resources or of communications so as to be able ultimately to confront the enemy with an offer of battle he would have to refuse. But in even the most marginal and ancillary of engagements, the destruction of the enemy force was what really mattered. This destruction was not simply *contributory* to the final objective of the strategist; it was in itself an *intrinsic part* of that objective. It was ultimately, to use another commercial analogy, the only thing that would show up on the final balance sheet of war.

In his closer analysis Clausewitz did something to soften the grimness of his presentation. 'Destruction of the enemy's forces' he defined more precisely as 'a reduction of strength relatively larger than one's own' (p. 230). Again he uses his commercial analogy. 'Only the direct profit gained in the process of mutual destruction may be considered as having been the object. This profit is absolute: it remains fixed throughout the entire balance sheet of the campaign and at the end will always prove pure gain.' But the destruction that mattered, he emphasized, was not physical but moral – the destruction of the enemy's capacity to resist, the 'killing of his courage rather than his men'. It was only after the enemy's morale had been broken that the balance tipped, and it became possible to inflict heavier losses on the enemy than one was suffering oneself. Losses during a battle consisted mainly of dead and wounded, and were normally shared fairly evenly between the two sides. After the battle they consisted of captured guns and prisoners, and 'that is why guns and prisoners have always counted as the real trophies of victory; they are also its measure, for they are tangible evidence of its scale' (p. 232).

This was true of all engagements, large or small, but the greater proportionate effect on enemy morale of the losses incurred in a major engagement was self-evident. Indeed if the destruction of the enemy main force was the strategist's object, whether it was simply, as Clausewitz put it, 'the best way to begin' or was an object 'that led directly to peace' (pp. 596, 143), then this was best achieved in a single concentrated great battle, a conflict which Clausewitz distinguished by the gruesome name *die Schlacht*, a word which in German also means 'slaughter'. To the *Schlacht* and its aftermath, the pursuit of the defeated army, Clausewitz devoted five consecutive chapters. In this kind of climactic encounter, as he described it, all individual engagements coalesced and were fought out under the personal direction of the commander-in-chief himself. It was concentrated war, a burning-glass focusing all its destructive potential on a single point in time and space. Unlike other, subordinate engagements it was not a means to a further end; it was the end in itself and contained within itself its own purpose.

In his description of such a battle Clausewitz abandoned his tone of cool, dispassionate analysis and wrote with a passion to be found nowhere else in the work. Understandably: the *Schlacht* was the central feature of Napoleonic warfare, and he had himself been involved in no less than three – the catastrophe of Jena, the bloody draw of Borodino and the victorious but hard-fought climax of La Belle Alliance, better known to the British as Waterloo. This was war at its most intense, something the old formal strategists (and the new ones) had never comprehended, and Clausewitz was determined to drive it home. Much of the writing is clearly autobiographical, as in this description of a commander recognizing the onset of a defeat:

> The loss of entire batteries while none are captured from the enemy; the crushing of his battalions by the enemy's cavalry while the enemy's own battalions remain impenetrable; the involuntary retreat of his firing line from point to point; futile efforts to capture certain positions, which end in the scattering of the assault troops by well-aimed grape and case-shot; a weakening of the rate of fire of his guns as opposed to the enemy's; an abnormally rapid thinning-out of his battalions under fire caused by groups of able-bodied men accompanying the wounded to the rear; units cut off and captured because the battle line is disrupted; evidence of the line of retreat being imperilled; all this will indicate to a commander where he and his battle are heading. (p. 250)

Clausewitz is scrupulously fair in reminding us that although a *Schlacht* was a decisive factor in a war or a campaign, it was 'not necessarily the only one. Campaigns whose outcome have been determined by a single battle have been fairly common only in recent times, and those cases in which they have settled an entire war are very rare exceptions' (p. 260). None the less, the stress laid on the *Schlacht*, the space devoted to it, and the emotional quality of the writing, all suggest that he regarded a campaign that culminated in such an encounter as somehow morally superior to one that did not, that bloodless victory was only for eunuchs. 'We are not interested in generals who win victories without bloodshed. The fact that slaughter is a horrifying spectacle must make us take war more seriously, but not provide an excuse for gradually blunting our swords in the name of humanity. Sooner or later someone will come along with a sharp sword and hack off our arms' (p. 260).

In the framework of his whole argument, and against the background of a contrary strategic doctrine which had brought disaster on his own country, Clausewitz's reasoning is as flawless as his passion is understandable. Taken out of their context, such passages as these give a horrifying impression of Clausewitz's teaching, but no one who had experienced Napoleonic warfare could have quarrelled with his statement 'the character of battle is slaughter, and its price is blood' (p. 259). He was determined not to let his readers ever lose sight of the horrible reality that lay at the centre of the urbane, abstract, or technical treatises in which every strategic analyst before him, and all too many of them since, dealt with the subject of war. This was not the least of the services he rendered to soldiers and civilians alike.

Chapter 4
Limited and absolute war

The distinction which Clausewitz drew between 'limited' and 'absolute' (or 'total') war, and which twentieth-century political and strategic thinkers have found so significant, did not emerge as the result of any long and profound thought. He was, as we have already seen, only 24 when he first stated that wars could be of two kinds, those fought for the elimination of the opponent's political independence (*seine Staatenexistenz aufzuheben*) and those fought to obtain favourable terms of peace. There is no indication that either he or anyone else at the time saw anything remarkable in the idea. But in a note written in 1827, twenty-three years later, when he had been at work on *On War* for a dozen years and had drafted three-quarters of the book, Clausewitz wrote that it was now necessary for him to go over the whole thing again to 'bring out the two types of war with greater clarity at every point' (p. 69). So although the distinction between the two must have always been in his mind, as for anyone who had experienced both the wars of the eighteenth century and those of Bonaparte, the fundamental importance of this dichotomy for his theory only struck him as he was writing. To be precise, it seems to have struck him halfway through the sixth book of *On War*, that on Defence, when he realized that here more than anywhere else the commander needed to know whether he was fighting 'the kind of war that is completely governed and saturated by the urge for a decision', or one that approximated rather to 'a war of observation' (pp. 488–9). Why this distinction was particularly important in planning a defensive campaign we shall see later in this chapter.

Clausewitz considered it necessary for his reader not only to appreciate that there were two types of war, but to understand exactly why this should be so. In fact he provided three distinct explanations: one historical, or sociological; one metaphysical; and one empirical. Each occurs in a different section of *On War*, and is set out with little relation to the other two. They were not indeed entirely mutually compatible.

Historically, Clausewitz pointed out, all wars were the products of the societies that fought them. Like all other institutions war was shaped by the ideas, the emotions, and conditions prevailing at the time. How this had affected the development of warfare he explained in what must have been the earliest survey of the sociology of war from the earliest times to his own day. Having described how war was made and supported by the Tatar hordes, the republics of antiquity, the Roman Empire, the political authorities of the Middle Ages, and the *condottieri* of the early modern period, he focused on the development of the sovereign states of eighteenth-century Europe. By then, he showed, monarchs had obtained such effective political and economic control over the peoples they ruled that they were able to create war machines distinct and separate from the rest of society, regular armies with their own sources of finance and supply which monarchs controlled so completely that they were able to behave 'as if they were themselves the State'. But these resources were finite.

> Their means of waging war came to consist of the money in their coffers and of such idle vagabonds as they could lay their hands on either at home or abroad ... If the army was pulverised, he could not raise another, and behind the army there was nothing. That enjoined the greatest prudence in all operations ... Armies, with their fortresses and prepared positions, came to form a state within a state, in which violence gradually faded away. (pp. 589–90)

The development of civilized social mores and of a political system so closely integrated that 'no cannon could be fired in Europe without every government feeling its interest affected' further enforced the limitations on both the means of conducting war and the objectives for which it was fought. But the French Revolution changed everything. 'Suddenly war again became the business of the people – a people of thirty millions, all of whom considered themselves to be citizens' (p. 592).

> War, untrammelled by any conventional restraints, had broken loose in all its elemental fury. This was due to the peoples' new share in these great affairs of state; and their participation, in its turn, resulted partly from the impact that the Revolution had on the internal conditions of every state and partly from the danger that France posed to everyone. (p. 593)

Whether this transformation was likely to be permanent Clausewitz was too cautious, and perhaps too politically shrewd, to say; though he warned that 'once barriers – which in a sense consist only of man's ignorance of what is possible – are torn down, they are not easily set up again'. The important point for his theory was that 'each age had in its own kind of war, its own limiting conditions, and its own peculiar preconceptions'. It was these cultural circumstances that determined whether war would be total or limited, and what the limits would be.

When he started to revise *On War*, however, Clausewitz adopted a different approach. In the first chapter of the first book, which may in fact have been the last complete chapter that he wrote and was certainly the only one with which he professed himself satisfied, Clausewitz presented the concept of 'absolute war' not as something culturally conditioned but as a Platonic ideal, to which most wars in reality were imperfect approximations. It was 'ideal', that is, in the sense not of being 'good', but of being logical and (in the Aristotelian

51

sense) 'natural'. The intrinsic *nature* of war, that is, was total. It was 'an act of force, and there is no logical limit to an act of force' (p. 77). This statement Clausewitz justified by the concept of what he called 'reciprocal action' and which today we would term 'escalation'. The object in war is to impose your will on the enemy – it is *'an act of force to compel our enemy to do our will'* (p. 75). You cannot do this unless you destroy the enemy's power to resist; for if you do not render him powerless, he will try to render you powerless in his turn. So long as he has any capacity for resistance left, therefore, you are logically bound, in self-defence, to try to destroy it: there is no stopping-place short of the extreme.

That this rarely if ever happened in reality was due, according to Clausewitz, to a host of factors extraneous to the war itself. War was never a self-contained activity, consisting of a single decisive act or a series of simultaneous acts occurring in a political vacuum, unrelated to the events that had led up to it or to the situation it was intended to produce. The intentions of the belligerents and the course of the war were shaped by such considerations as the international environment, the pre-war relationship of the belligerent powers, the characteristics of the armed forces, the terrain of the theatre of war, and perceptions of the new situation that it was hoped the war would produce. These, far more than any requirements of military logic, determined how the war should be fought. Clausewitz denied indeed that war could have its own logic; it could only, he said, have its own grammar.

War came about, Clausewitz insisted, because of a *political situation*. 'The occasion is always due to some political object', he wrote: 'War is therefore an act of policy' (p. 607). Policy was the guiding intelligence, war only the instrument. But even this was a misleading analogy. War could not be considered as existing distinct from policy, however subordinate it might be to it. It was part of policy, a mode of it, a continuation of political intercourse (*Verkehr*) with the addition of other means.

We deliberately use the phrase 'with the addition of other means' because we also want to make it clear that war in itself does not suspend political intercourse or change it into something entirely different . . . The main lines along which military events progress, and to which they are restricted, are political lines that continue throughout the war into the subsequent peace . . . War cannot be divorced from political life; and whenever this occurs in our thinking about war, the many links that connect the two elements are destroyed and we are left with something pointless and devoid of sense. (p. 605)

This formulation has taken us a long way from the simple concept of 'the two types of war'. Given that considerations of policy are paramount, and knowing that the requirements of policy may be almost infinitely various, war can surely be of *any* kind, not only of two. It might be, as Clausewitz put it, a 'terrible two-handed battlesword' capable of settling matters at a single stroke, or it might be 'a harmless foil fit only for thrusts and feints and parries' (p. 606). But it might also be anything in between.

The implications of this possibility of gradation, as opposed to the sharp distinction between two categories, Clausewitz did not live to explore. He never really considered the territory that lay between his two 'models'. But he did make the point, one vividly present to the mind of any survivor of the Jena campaign, that it took two to fight a limited war. If your opponent was prepared to exert himself to the utmost to achieve his objective, you had no choice but to do the same. The logical escalation to 'absolute war' had then to be accepted. For that reason, he insisted, the strategist must always have the ideal of absolute war clearly in mind. You had to approximate to the ideal form 'when you can and when you must' (p. 581).

According to this formulation, then, the nature of war was determined not so much by cultural circumstances as by the reasoned decisions of the political leaders who called the war into being. But Clausewitz advanced yet a third explanation for the limited nature of most wars, this one intrinsic to the conduct of war itself.

Clausewitz was obviously fascinated by a paradox in the conduct of war to which he reverted again and again – something he termed 'the suspension of the action'. In principle one might expect to find that war was a matter of continuous, violent, and mutually murderous activity. In practice armies, even at the height of a campaign, often spent most of their time sitting around doing nothing. It was one of those insights into the realities of military life that place Clausewitz in a class of his own as a military analyst, for it really is this tedious inactivity, quite as much as the element of 'friction', that distinguishes the reality of war from the neat models of the strategic theorist. War, as it has been well said, consists of nine parts boredom to one of fear.

Clausewitz's explanation of this phenomenon was initially linked to his analysis of the interaction between attack and defence. It was seldom, he pointed out, that both sides *simultaneously* had a strong incentive to take the initiative. (One of the few occasions when this did happen was at the outbreak of the Great War in 1914, when all the major belligerents launched offensive operations.) However offensive the intentions of both belligerents might be, it was unlikely that both would choose the same moment to attack. One side might want to wait until it had built up its strength, and so remained for the time being on the defensive. That defensive posture, in its turn, might appear so formidable as to deter its opponent from attacking, so that he also decided to wait for a better moment. As a result nothing very much might happen for quite a long time.

Human nature being what it is, went on Clausewitz, this was the case more often than not. Information about the enemy was uncertain, and one was always more likely to overestimate than to underestimate the opponent's strength. 'The fear and indecision native to the human mind' thus weighed everyone down, constituting a kind of 'moral force of gravity . . . In the fiery climate of war, ordinary natures tend to move more ponderously: stronger and more frequent stimuli are therefore needed to ensure that momentum is maintained' (p. 217). However extreme and 'absolute' the political object of the war might be, it could not in itself overcome this 'ponderousness'. 'Unless an enterprising martial spirit is in command,' maintained Clausewitz, 'a man who is as much at home in war as a fish is in water . . . inactivity will be the rule, and progress the exception.'

If there was no such 'martial spirit' to provide an impetus, no popular pressures involved and no great goals in view, a campaign was likely to make slower and slower progress. War became 'something half-hearted' (p. 218) as it had been in the eighteenth century, and came to resemble nothing so much as a *Spiel*, a game of chance. We have seen how the element of hazard and luck gave something of this quality to all wars, but without political or popular motivation and in the absence of a bold commander war resembled not so much a play for high stakes as 'haggling over small change'. It was when this happened, said Clausewitz, that the minor skills of the generals of the rococo period, their feints and manœuvres and ambushes, acquired an exaggerated importance and were wrongly – and disastrously – believed to constitute the entire art of war.

According to this explanation. then, even if the nature of war in the abstract was something absolute, the nature of the men who fought the wars constrained it and made it fall short of its *Vollkommenheit*, its 'perfection'. Perhaps war *should* be limited, or at least determined, by its political objective; but certainly it *would* be limited, or at least constrained, by human weakness, by the intrinsic element of 'friction'. In order to achieve the objectives of even a limited war it would be necessary to make efforts above the ordinary – to take the model of 'absolute war' as one's target. So although the fighting of an 'absolute war' was only one, and perhaps the least common, of the possible demands that statesmen were likely to make on the military, the military commander had to keep it in sight as an ideal if he was to fight even limited wars of policy effectively; 'to approximate to it when he can and when he must' (p. 58). With that it might be thought there went the corollary, as Bismarck was to discover a generation later, that the statesman needed to keep a sharp eye on the soldier if the latter was not to overshoot the mark and turn a limited war into an absolute one. But this was an aspect of the matter that Clausewitz failed to consider.

I have made the point that the full importance of this distinction between the two types of war dawned on Clausewitz not when he was writing one of his more analytic chapters, but in the middle of the very long section, full of detailed topographical and tactical information, that he devoted to defence. It is a book that editors of potted versions of Clausewitz often and understandably prefer to omit, but in doing so they deprive their readers of much of the essence of Clausewitz's thought. In particular the prescriptive elements in his work, the specific proposals for the conduct of a campaign which he lays down in his final book 'On War Plans', can be understood only in the light of the principles he worked out in meditating about the defence – something he did so comprehensively that it left him with very little to add in the subsequent section, on 'The Attack'.

Clausewitz began by making two points about the defence. First, although its object was negative, it was a *stronger* form of war than the attack. It was easier to hold ground than to take it, to preserve than to acquire. A weaker force, unless it was desperate, did not attack a stronger one; it stayed on the defensive and made up for its weakness by maximizing the advantages of a defensive position. *Beati sunt possidentes*, said Clausewitz: blessed are those in possession, in war as in law.

But defence could not be purely passive. Clausewitz's second point was that defence essentially consisted of two phases: *waiting* for a blow and *parrying* it (*Abwehr*). This latter action, this counterblow against the attacker, was intrinsic to the whole concept of defence. An army took up defensive positions in order to *fight* from them. It selected them in order to maximize its fighting effectiveness, not least that of its fire power. A defence was a shield, said Clausewitz, but an *active* shield, one 'made up of well-directed blows' (p. 357). You did not just sit behind your defences and let the attack overwhelm you: you fired back. It was usually the defender, indeed, who fired the first shot in any war. As Clausewitz put it, in a passage which gained the sardonic approval of Lenin:

> The aggressor is always peace-loving (as Bonaparte always claimed to be); he would prefer to take over our country unopposed. To prevent his doing so one must be willing to make war and be prepared for it. In other words it is the weak, those most likely to need defence, who should always be armed in order not to be overwhelmed. (p. 370)

A defensive strategy consisted in finding the right balance between these two elements, waiting and parrying; of choosing the right time and place to unleash that 'flashing sword of vengeance' which Clausewitz described as 'the greatest moment for the defender'. There was a whole range of possibilities open, from an immediate counter-attack the moment the enemy crossed the frontier – minimum waiting, immediate riposte – to a long withdrawal into the interior of the country such as the Russians had carried out in 1812 and were to do again in 1941 and 1942, delaying until the last possible moment before launching their counter-attack. All depended, said Clausewitz, whether one wanted primarily to destroy the enemy by one's own forces, or by 'his own exertions' (p. 384).

In this latter strategy of delayed riposte Clausewitz assumed that the advantages lay with the defender, who was falling back along his own supply lines amid a friendly population, rather than with his assailant, whose supply problems grew greater, his forces weaker, and the environment more hostile the further he advanced. Eventually the balance of advantage would tip, when the attacker had touched his lowest point of weakness and the defender had amassed his optimum strength. This moment Clausewitz described as the 'culminating point' when the flashing sword of vengeance should be drawn and the counter-attack unleashed. The skill of the strategist lay in discerning when the right moment had come.

It can be argued that in making this analysis Clausewitz allowed himself to be unduly influenced by the campaign of 1812. There had after all been several campaigns in his own lifetime, not least those of 1805 and 1806, when the advancing army had not been enervated by its progress but had drawn moral encouragement from it, when the retreating forces had been increasingly demoralized as they abandoned more and more of their territory to the enemy, and when the assailant had been able to solve his supply problems at his adversary's expense. There are also few countries in Europe whose defenders have the opportunity to withdraw very far into the interior without abandoning terrain or resources vital to the fighting of the war. But where the opportunity does exist it can certainly be used very effectively, as successive invaders of Russia have discovered to their cost. And even in the restricted theatre of Northern France in 1914 Joffre was able to let the German armies largely defeat themselves 'by their own exertions' before unleashing his 'flashing sword of vengeance' on the Marne.

In any case Clausewitz described how prolongation of the defence by a carefully planned and hard-fought withdrawal might make available an increasing range of resources. In the first place, given the existing political system in Europe and the general preference among its rulers for the maintenance of the balance of power, neutral states were likely to redress the balance by coming to the help of the victim of aggression: again, an optimistic assessment, not entirely borne out by the historical record. In the second place, there were the resources afforded by the environment, the natural ones of terrain and the artificial ones created by military engineers, all of which he analysed with great expertise. And finally there was the support of the people themselves – the factor left out of account by all strategists before Clausewitz and most of them since.

Clausewitz had written elsewhere in *On War* about the relationship of regular armies to popular forces, and the strengths and weaknesses of the latter. It was a matter about which his experience and activities, especially during the winter of 1812–13 when he was organizing popular resistance in East Prussia, uniquely qualified him to speak. In the section on defence Clausewitz included a chapter dealing specifically with guerrilla warfare, 'The People in Arms'. It was a topic about which, he admitted, there was very little information: 'this sort of warfare is not as yet very common [and] those who have been able to observe it for any length of time have not reported enough about it' (p. 483). It was also a controversial issue, both among military men who claimed that it was a waste of resources and more generally among those who saw in popular insurrection 'a state of legalised anarchy that is as much a threat to the social order at home as it is to the enemy' (p. 479). To the former, Clausewitz pointed out that the resources used in guerrilla warfare would probably not be available for any other purpose. As for the latter, he reminded them that popular insurrections had to be seen as part of the general erosion of conventional barriers, 'a broadening and intensification of the fermentation process known as war' which was so characteristic of the times. Like other novel forms of warfare, 'any nation that uses it intelligently will, as a rule, gain some superiority over those who disdain its use'. 'If this is so, the question only remains whether mankind at large will gain by this further expansion of the element of war; a question to which the answer should be the same as to the question of war itself. We shall leave both to the philosophers' (p. 479).

The questions that Clausewitz here raised have been hotly debated down to our own day. But Clausewitz, unlike some later theorists, never considered guerrilla war in isolation. For him it was one more resource in the spectrum of defence capabilities, and it could be realistically considered only 'within the framework of a war conducted by the regular army, and coordinated in one all-encompassing plan' (p. 480). Such a plan could provide for popular insurrection either as an auxiliary activity before a decisive battle or as a last resort after a defeat. In either case, argued Clausewitz, one should never flinch from making use of it.

> A government must never assume that its country's fate, its whole existence, depends on a single battle, no matter how decisive ... No matter how small and weak a state may be in comparison with its enemy, it must not forego these last efforts, or one would conclude that its soul is dead. They are even more desirable when help can be expected from other states that have an interest in our survival. A government that after having lost a major battle is only interested in letting its people go back to sleep as soon as possible, and, overwhelmed by feelings of failure and disappointment, lacks the courage and desire to put forth a final effort is, because of its weakness, involved in a major inconsistency in any case. It shows that it did not deserve to win, and possibly for that very reason was unable to. (p. 483)

This passage, which epitomizes much of his political writings, helps explain why Clausewitz was so unpopular with the cautious and conservative advisers of Frederick William III.

But what if the enemy was not concerned to overthrow your State but had, on the contrary, the kind of limited objectives so common in the eighteenth century – the occupation of some frontier provinces, either to annexe them or to use them as hostages in peace negotiations? What if his attack was a secondary operation ancillary to a more decisive thrust elsewhere? What if he attacked only half-heartedly at the behest of a major ally from whom, with skilful management, he might be detached? This would involve a very different kind of defensive strategy. A withdrawal into the interior, the stripping of frontier defences so as to concentrate forces for a major and decisive battle, then became a quite

60

inappropriate plan. The correct strategy would then be to hold on to as much territory as possible for as long as possible. It was therefore essential that, in making his dispositions, the strategist should know what kind of a war he was going to have to fight. Was it a 'greater or lesser approximation to a war of observation', or was it, on the contrary, one 'completely governed and saturated by the urge for a decision' (p. 488)? This overall political consideration would from the very outset determine his military plans.

It was at this point, in chapter 28 of Book VI of *On War*, that Clausewitz began to treat the two types of war as presenting quite distinct problems to the commander; something he had not yet done anywhere in the work, and which he was not now to have the time adequately to do. In the final book (VIII) 'On War Plans' the two kinds of war were to be carefully distinguished and the appropriate strategic principles for each prescribed in some detail. The first part of that book was taken up with that mature discussion about the primacy of the political object that we have already described and for which Clausewitz is probably most widely known. It was only when his mind was clear on this fundamental point that Clausewitz began the redraft of the entire work that he never lived to complete.

Chapter 5
The legacy of Clausewitz

Clausewitz's modest ambition to write a work that 'would not be forgotten after two or three years' at first showed little sign of being fulfilled. The edition of his works that his widow published in 1832, the year after his death, was received with respect but made little impact. In 1867 a survey of military literature in Europe made the damning comment that Clausewitz was 'well-known but little read'. *On War* might have been a forgotten curiosity had not Helmuth von Moltke, the acknowledged architect of Prussia's military triumphs over Austria and France and so, with Bismarck, the creator of the united German Empire in 1871, let it be known in the aftermath of his triumph that, apart from the Bible and Homer, Clausewitz was the author whose work had influenced him most.

With Moltke's endorsement, Clausewitz instantly became fashionable. In 1873 a German military journal, taking its cue from the top, pronounced that 'Clausewitz has earned his place as the foremost authority on military learning in the German army'. The wars of 1866 and 1870, it said, had shown how 'strong discipline, good weapons, appropriate elementary tactics, good march dispositions, railways, practical supply arrangements and communications determine everything in war. This purely craftsmanlike concept which is so widespread in the army and has effected such a transformation, is the consequence of Clausewitz's ingenious destructive activity.'

What Clausewitz had destroyed was the formalistic strategy of manœuvre that had been generally taught in staff colleges before 1870, its dominance assisted by the longevity of the influential Jomini, who died only at the age of 90 in 1869, and whose well-organized didactic textbooks had been translated into every major European language. Jomini's teaching directly moulded the doctrines of the French, the Russian, and the American Armies, and through his influence on W. von Willisen in Prussia and E. B. Hamley in England much of the thinking of those armies as well. 'But for Clausewitz, Jomini would probably have been Moltke's guiding spirit', wrote a later authority, Rudolf von Caemmerer, with something like horror: '[He] freed us from all that artificiality which gave itself such airs in the theory of war and has shown us what, after all, is the real point.'

Moltke had been a pupil at the War College in Clausewitz's time, but had no contact with him there, and according to his biographer Eberhard Kessel there is little evidence from his diaries and letters that he had studied his work very deeply. Clausewitz's ideas about the importance of moral forces, the desirability of seeking out the enemy and destroying him by battle, the need for flexibility and self-reliance and concentration were fairly commonplace in the Prussian Army after 1815. Indeed they were particularly characteristic of the more liberal-thinking and forward-looking young officers of the time, in contrast to the formalistic strategic concepts being reimposed by the conservative hierarchy. Moltke only absorbed from Clausewitz and passed on to his own disciples those ideas that coincided with his own. The image of Clausewitz that was transmitted to the German Army, and indeed to the world in the latter half of the nineteenth century, was transmitted through Moltke almost as totally as the image of Marx was transmitted to the Russian peoples through Lenin. It was not inaccurate but it was distorted and very incomplete.

Moltke's own writings echo Clausewitz to the point of plagiarism.

Victory through the application of armed force is the decisive factor in war. Victory alone breaks the will of the enemy and compels him to submit to ours. It is not the occupation of a slice of territory or the capture of a fortress but the destruction of enemy forces that will decide the outcome of the war. This destruction thus constitutes the principal object of operations.

It is a mistake to believe that one can lay down a plan of campaign and follow it through point by point from beginning to end. The first encounter with the main enemy will create . . . an entirely new situation. To appreciate precisely the changes which events have effected on the situation, take the desired measures in a relatively short time and execute them with all desirable resolution is all the General Staff can do.

Strategic doctrine hardly extends beyond the first principles of common sense . . . Its value lies almost wholly in its concrete application.

In war it is less important what one does than how one does it. Strong determination and perseverance in carrying through a simple idea are the surest route to one's objective.

These ideas were disseminated by a whole generation of German strategic writers in the two decades after 1870, many of whom had served on Moltke's staff. 'It would be to misunderstand the nature of strategy to try to transform it into a predetermined scientific system', wrote one of the most eminent, Verdy du Vernois, '. . . Precision in conception, energy in the execution of one's plan, these are the pilots most capable of steering us through all the reefs.' And this simplicity in planning, this energy in execution, had to be complemented by a readiness at all levels to take responsibility. 'Everyone', wrote Verdy, 'must hold the conviction that it is better to advance on one's own responsibility than to remain idle, waiting for orders.' All of which led Verdy and his generation to the conclusion that 'military qualities are rooted rather in character than in knowledge': a perfect Clausewitzian formulation, and one which professional military men have loudly echoed ever since.

This was the selection of Clausewitzian ideas that dominated the German Army at the beginning of the twentieth century. The French took a little longer to discover the virtues of their enemy's principal mentor, but by 1900 there was in the French Army what has been described as 'a veritable craze [*engouement*] for Clausewitz'. There were those who maintained that Clausewitz was only expressing with typical teutonic obscurity what Napoleon had stated with far greater clarity and force, but the whole emphasis upon 'moral forces' fitted in perfectly not only with the traditions of the French Army itself, antedating the Revolution and recently reinforced by its experience of colonial warfare, but with the philosophy of *élan vital* which was being made fashionable by the philosopher Henri Bergson (1859–1941). Clausewitz's most influential disciple in France was the future Marshal Ferdinand Foch, whose *Principles of War*, published in 1903, contained virtually an abstract (not always acknowledged) of Clausewitz's views. Defeat, he there argued, 'is in fact a purely moral result, that of a mood of discouragement, of terror, wrought in the soul of the conquered by the combined use of moral and material factors simultaneously resorted to by the victor'. It was not a bad diagnosis, as was to be borne out by the events of September 1914 when General Joffre, in spite of having suffered defeats on the frontiers that made the battles of 1870 look like small-scale skirmishes, kept his head, refused to be panicked and counter-attacked on the Marne; something that his successor in 1940, General Gamelin, notably failed to do.

But Joffre's initial defeats had been due to imprudent and premature *offensives*, and in launching those offensives he was only doing the same as every other general in Europe. How did Clausewitz's disciples in 1914 reconcile their admiration for his teaching with their ignoring of his explicit doctrine that defence was the stronger form of war – a doctrine which the development of firearms since Clausewitz's death had so powerfully reinforced? Moltke himself had taken this seriously into account even in the 1860s, developing a doctrine of 'strategic offensive, tactical defensive' to enable his infantry to maximize the advantages of their new breech-loading rifles. Forty years later, when rifles had not only tripled their range, accuracy, and rate of fire but been reinforced by machine-guns, Foch found arguments in other pages of *On War* to justify his belief in the superiority of the offensive.

> To fall on, but to fall on in *numbers*, in *masses*: therein lies salvation. For numbers, provided we know how to use them, will allow us, by means of the physical superiority placed at our disposal, to get the better of the violent enemy fire. Having more guns we will silence his own; it is the same with rifles, the same with bayonets, if we know how to use them all.

The best strategy in short was to be very strong; first generally and then at the decisive point.

Clausewitz's teaching about the primacy of the defensive was regarded by pre-1914 strategists as an embarrassment, to be ignored or explained away. His biographer von Caemmerer wrote in 1905, of his definition of defence as 'the stronger form with the negative object', that 'the more or less keen opposition to this sentence never ceases'. The most widely read of all German strategic writers, Colmar von der Goltz, in his popular work *The Nation in Arms* (1883), argued that if Clausewitz had lived to revise his text he would have changed his mind on this point, since it was incompatible with his teaching about the destruction of the enemy. 'He who stays on the defensive does not make war, he endures it', argued von der Goltz; '. . . Happy the soldier to whom fate assigns the part of the assailant!'

Strategists before 1914 were in fact increasingly hypnotized by the Clausewitzian and Napoleonic idea of the decisive battle for the overthrow of the enemy, that *Vernichtungsschlacht* to which Clausewitz had devoted so many pages. So not only was Clausewitz's teaching about the primacy of the defensive abandoned, but also the idea, even more central to his theory, of the two types of war. Any possibility that war in Europe could be anything other than total had by 1900 become discounted. Von der Goltz expressed a view general among his countrymen when he wrote:

> If two European Powers of the first order collide, their whole organised forces will at once be set in motion to decide the quarrel. All political considerations, bred of the half-heartedness of wars of alliance, will fall to the ground . . . All moral energy will be gathered for a life and death struggle, the whole sum of the intelligence residing in either people will be employed for their mutual destruction.

And that this was not a purely German view one can see by turning to Foch: 'You must henceforward go to the very limits to find the object of war. Since the vanquished party never now yields before it has been deprived of all means of reply, what you have to aim at is the destruction of those means of reply.'

But if war was henceforth to be total, what became of Clausewitz's dogma that it was only an instrument of policy and that the military leadership must take its cue from its political leaders? This was an aspect of Clausewitz's teaching too basic for anyone to ignore, and the rivalry between Moltke and Bismarck over the direction of strategy in 1870 had provided a notorious example of the problems that it created. Goltz did not ignore it, but he found an ingenious solution:

> War is always the servant of policy . . . without a sound policy, success in war is improbable. War will on that account be in no way lowered in importance . . . if only the commander in chief and the leading statesmen are agreed that *in all circumstances war serves the ends of politics best by a complete defeat of the enemy.*

That left the statesmen little choice. The same view was being expressed decades later beyond the Rhine by the French military historian Jean Colin, whose book *The Transformations of War* was published in 1911:

> The mutual conditions of modern war no longer admit of avoidance of the radical decision by battle. The two armies occupying the whole area of the theatre of operations march towards each other, and there is no issue but victory. Therefore the indications which a government should give to a general on the political object of war are reduced to a very small affair. Once the war is decided upon, it is absolutely necessary that a general should be left free to conduct it at his own discretion, subject to seeing himself relieved of his command if he uses his discretion with but little energy and competence.

All these prophecies were to be self-fulfilling. The social and material conditions of Europe in the early twentieth century had indeed produced armed forces for whom the fighting of 'limited wars' was simply not possible. Even if the activities of these armies had been susceptible to the kind of fine tuning that Clausewitz had so admired in Frederick the Great, 'the passions of the peoples', that third element in Clausewitz's 'remarkable trinity', would have made it impossible. The spread of democratic ideas had made nations more bellicose rather than less and had, as Clausewitz had foretold, increased the totality of the wars they fought, bringing them nearer to his idea of 'absolute war'. Clausewitz's critics, such as Liddell Hart, were later to blame his influence for the destructive way in which the First World War was conducted, especially on the Western Front; for the lack of subtlety in strategic thinking, the implacable determination of military leaders to gain their objectives whatever the cost, their almost joyful acceptance of heavy casualties as an indication not of military incompetence but of moral strength. Clausewitz's defenders could reply that, given the issues that were seen to be at stake, the war could only be settled by just such a 'trial of moral and physical forces by means of the latter', and

68

no amount of military skill could have attained the political objects –
the preservation or destruction of the Habsburg Empire, the
establishment or prevention of a German hegemony in Europe, the
maintenance of British maritime supremacy, and the territorial integrity
of France – any more cheaply. But Clausewitz himself might have
reminded us of those passages in which he related the conduct of war to
its social environment, pointing out how

> every age had its own kind of war, its own limiting conditions, and its
> own peculiar preconceptions . . . It follows therefore that the events of
> every age must be judged in the light of its own peculiarities. One cannot
> therefore understand and appreciate the commanders of the past until
> one has placed oneself in the situation of their times. (p. 593)

The First World War was conducted as it was, not because the major
military figures happened to have read Clausewitz, but because it was
so determined by the social and political structure of their epoch.
Clausewitz's prescription for the conduct of war, certainly as interpreted
through Moltke and his disciples, is indeed open to legitimate criticism,
but his descriptive analysis can hardly be faulted.

This, of course, was the aspect of Clausewitz's teaching that had so
impressed Marx and Engels, and was to influence in their turn both
Lenin and Trotsky. War was an instrument of policy and policy was the
product of certain basic social factors that had to be grasped before any
valid military doctrine could be worked out. The tenets of Marxist-
Leninism, it was and is believed, made possible a scientific insight into
these 'objective factors'. The frequent and flattering references to
Clausewitz that are to be found in Lenin's writings were to make his
ideas acceptable to Marxist-Leninists in spite of his bourgeois militarist
background, much as Aquinas's homage to Aristotle made that pagan
philosopher acceptable to the medieval Church. The new army
reconstituted by the Soviet Union after the Revolution and the Civil War
thus took the Clausewitzian doctrine about the relationship of war to

policy as the foundation for its own military thinking; and few Soviet military textbooks did not contain at least a passing reference to it.

In the West however after 1918 this aspect of Clausewitz's teaching was regarded as being as sinister as his strategic doctrine was disastrous. To British and American liberals the much-quoted and misquoted aphorism 'War is the continuation of policy by other means' was regarded not as a piece of serious political analysis but as shocking evidence of militaristic cynicism. As for his strategic doctrine, it was condemned especially strongly by British thinkers who believed that they had discovered a more effective and humane means of conducting war than through the blood-baths to which the uncritical acceptance of Clausewitz's teaching by continental theorists appeared to have led.

Even before 1914 the absence from Clausewitz's work of any consideration of maritime or economic war had been noted and criticized in Britain. Soon after the beginning of the century, however, the growing possibility of a war with Germany set on foot the moral and material preparation of the British Army for participation in large-scale warfare on the Continent for the first time since 1815. A study both of French and of German writings about continental warfare led such British military writers as Spenser Wilkinson and F. N. Maude straight back to Clausewitz. *On War*, which had first been translated in 1873, was republished in 1908 to the accompaniment of many laudatory commentaries. By 1914 the British military leadership was no less impregnated than its continental contemporaries with a belief in the supremacy of moral forces, the need to seek out the enemy's centre of gravity in his army and defeat it in a decisive battle, whatever the cost. Like their continental contemporaries they also believed that the battle, though bloody, would be brief; and when events proved them wrong they settled down to the grim slogging match that followed with all the calm determination that Clausewitz prescribed for his commanders, ignoring the siren songs of those who argued that there might be a less painful road to victory and supposed it possible 'for a particularly ingenious method of inflicting minor direct damage on the enemy's forces to lead to major indirect destruction' (p. 228).

For this was precisely the claim made by critics of Britain's Western Front strategy, both at the time and since. Before 1914 the naval historian Julian Corbett had suggested that over the centuries the British had developed a 'maritime strategy' that was quite distinct from the Clausewitzian continental strategy. This consisted in using naval power both to bring direct economic pressure on a continental adversary, and to make limited military interventions on the Continent, as Wellington had done in the Peninsula during the Napoleonic Wars, with effects that could be out of all proportion to their size. This was the strategy advocated before the war by the naval authorities as against that of immediate and full-scale continental intervention favoured by the Army. It was rejected. But when at the end of 1914 the battles in the West ended in deadlock, it was revived and put into effect with the Dardanelles campaign, which was indeed seen by its authors as 'a particularly ingenious method of inflicting minor direct damage on the enemy's forces [so as] to lead to major indirect destruction'.

The tactical failure at the Dardanelles makes it impossible to judge whether the 'indirect' strategy it was meant to serve would have produced the results expected of it. At all events, the cost imposed by the return to a 'continental' strategy for the remainder of the war left a general impression, which grew stronger with the passage of years, that there *must* have been a more humane and economical way of obtaining victory; an impression crystallized by the teaching of the writer B. H. Liddell Hart, whose writings on *The Strategy of the Indirect Approach* and *The British Way in Warfare* were both widely read and highly influential on the formulation of British policy in the 1930s. So whereas in the Soviet Union Clausewitz was elevated to the strategic pantheon and in Germany he remained a deeply revered figure (indeed in the Nazi era he was almost idolized), in Britain his teachings fell into a neglect from which they have only recently begun to recover.

The major strategic innovation of the inter-war years was the development of air power. The theorists who pressed for its development used Clausewitzian arguments, but few mentioned his name. They started with his concept of 'the centre of gravity'. The experience of the First World War, they argued, had shown that the centre of gravity of a belligerent power was no longer to be found in his armed forces. The vital factor was now the morale of his civilian population. It had been the disintegration of the Home Front, not the defeat of their armed forces, that had caused the collapse, first of Russia, then of the Central Powers. Air power now made it possible to attack this centre of gravity directly. So it was against this 'hub of all power and movement, on which everything depends, that . . . all our energies should be directed' (p. 596).

The refusal of the older services to accept this claim, and the controversies that ensued, added to the unprecedented complexity of the decisions that had to be taken by the Allies during the course of the Second World War. This was a conflict that lent itself at every level to Clausewitzian analysis. On every side, save in Japan, there was complete political control of strategic decisions. Clausewitz would have approved the efforts of Hitler in the early years to use his armed forces as instruments of his policy, but would have noted how the unlimited nature of his objectives made the war a total one far beyond his capacity to wage. He would have commented on the importance of public opinion in the formulation of Allied strategy, and might have indicated how the strength of this, once aroused, made virtually inevitable the policy of 'unconditional surrender' and very difficult any readjustment of Western policy to protect its interests against the Soviet Union during the last year of the war. Democratic governments are ill-adapted to carry out the fine tuning that characterized the age of Frederick the Great. He would have noted with interest the problems that confronted the Allies in determining the enemy 'centre of gravity', and the decision by the American High Command in 1941 that it lay, not with their immediate enemy, Japan, but with that enemy's stronger ally, Germany.

Above all, he would have found plenty of justification for his argument about the desirability of being very strong; first everywhere and then at the decisive point. It was ultimately by the deployment of an overwhelming superiority of force that the war was to be won.

The advent of nuclear weapons did not at first introduce any fundamental transformation of strategic thinking. During the Second World War the conflict between the exponents of air power and the more traditional strategists had been resolved by the surface forces being used to seize territory from which air attacks could be launched against both Germany and Japan in such strength that ultimately not only the will but the very capacity of those powers to resist had been shattered. Both land and naval power was necessary to enable air power to operate, and so it was in the first few years of the nuclear era. American nuclear weapons could be delivered against the Soviet Union only from vulnerable manned bombers whose bases, especially those in Western Europe, had to be protected against land attack. It was only the development of thermonuclear weapons with their almost inconceivable capacity for mass destruction, and then that of inter-continental ballistic missiles, that introduced an entirely new possibility into the conduct of war, *making feasible the total destruction of the enemy's will to resist without first defeating his armed forces.*

This meant that 'absolute war' as defined by Clausewitz was no longer a Platonic ideal but a physical possibility. War *could* now consist of 'a single short blow'. In his prophetic words:

> If war consisted of one decisive act, or a set of simultaneous decisions, preparations would tend towards totality, because no omission could ever be rectified. The sole criterion for preparations which the world of reality could provide would be the measures taken by the adversary, so far as they are known; the rest would once more be reduced to abstract calculations. (p. 79)

This is a depressingly accurate description of nuclear strategy as it developed during the 'Cold War' of 1949–89. Clausewitz had maintained that such a situation could never arise because 'the very nature of the resources [available for war] and their employment means that they cannot all be deployed at the same moment. The resources in question are the fighting forces proper, the country with its physical features and population, and its allies.' It was the deployment of this complex range of resources that made war such a protracted and unpredictable activity, creating that element of friction and uncertainty that kept all efforts short of the absolute.

Now all those *internal* constraints on 'absolute war' were removed and its complete realization had for the first time become a practical possibility; not, as Clausewitz had expected, through the unchaining of popular passions (although it was certainly this that made the two World Wars such 'total wars') but because of the factor that neither he nor any other serious thinker of his era had ever considered: technology. Whereas in Clausewitz's day human effort had been necessary to *transcend* the limitations imposed on the conduct of war by the constraints of the real world, now that effort was needed to *impose* such limits.

Clausewitz himself, it will be recalled, had identified two constraints on absolute war. One was the internal braking mechanism imposed by friction. The other was the external one imposed by the political aim – both the political circumstances out of which the war arose and the political conditions it was intended to bring about. In nuclear as in any other kind of war, therefore, Clausewitz's advice remains good. 'No one starts a war – or rather, no one in his senses should do so – without first being clear in his mind what he intends to achieve by that war and how he intends to conduct it' (p. 579).

The political aim, the object (*Zweck*) of the war, was thus even more significant than it had been in Clausewitz's day. But whereas Clausewitz visualized the political object as something which, if sufficiently grandiose, would enable the commander to break through the barriers of human weakness that normally limited war; in the nuclear age the political object had to be kept in mind in order to impose limits on an activity whose destructiveness, left to itself, will rapidly escalate to extremes of a kind such as Clausewitz had never conceived.

This was the essence of the theory of nuclear deterrence. The assumption which underlies this theory is that no political object is sufficiently desirable to compensate for the nuclear devastation of one's homeland. It is thus possible to set on victory, in Clausewitz's words 'an unacceptably high cost' (p. 91). And here one should also note the relevance to the concept of nuclear deterrence of what Clausewitz had to say about *unfought* engagements being as significant in their effects as fought ones. Nuclear deterrence consists almost entirely in calculating the effects of unfought engagements. An effective deterrent posture thus imposes on one's adversary very stringent limitations on the political objectives that he is likely to seek to attain by military means, as well as on the means that he is likely to use in order to attain them.

Clausewitz's thinking was also relevant to the problems of nuclear war in another way. In any international conflict the immediate political object is likely to be the control of territory. Even if the fundamental causes are to be sought in ideological rivalries or fears for the balance of power, a territorial objective will almost certainly be adopted (as was Belgium by both Germany and Britain in the First World War) 'that will serve the political purpose and symbolise it in the peace negotiations' (p. 81). The war is thus likely to resolve itself into, even if it does not immediately arise out of, a struggle for the control of territory, whatever may be the broader implications that lie behind that struggle. So at once the traditional elements of *territory* and *armed forces* are reintroduced into strategic calculations, bringing back with them the twilit atmosphere of *friction*. And in that environment all the considerations analysed by Clausewitz would be as relevant as they were a century and a half – or a millennium and a half – ago.

But control over territory involves also control over the people who live there, and here again the Clausewitzian insights have a lasting relevance. The essence of his teaching about popular participation in war is not to be found in the famous chapter on 'The People in Arms' – which is almost always misleadingly quoted out of its context – but in what he had to say about the long-term political processes that were making such participation inevitable, whether one liked it or not. Peoples were less and less likely to allow their political destinies to be determined over their heads. Mao Zedong and the theorists of revolutionary warfare gave to this social dimension an overriding importance which perhaps it deserves only in the context of 'wars of national liberation'; but it is one that strategists under any circumstances ignore at their peril. In this respect Marxist military thinkers had a far more realistic grasp of the central issues than their opposite numbers, hypnotized as they were by technology and geopolitics, in the West. If the people themselves are not prepared if necessary to take part in the defence of their country, they cannot in the long run be protected; and if they are not prepared to acquiesce indefinitely in alien conquest, that conquest cannot in the long run be sustained.

So it is as well to conclude where Clausewitz did himself, with his depiction of war as a 'remarkable trinity'

> composed of primordial violence, hatred and enmity, which are to be regarded as a blind natural force; of the play of chance and probability within which the creative spirit is free to roam; and of its element of subordination as an instrument of policy, which makes it subject to reason alone. The first of these three aspects mainly concerns the people; the second the commander and his army; the third the government . . .

These three tendencies are like three different codes of law, deep-rooted in their subject and yet variable in their relationship to one another. *A theory that ignores any one of them or seeks to fix an arbitrary relationship between them would conflict with reality to such an extent that for this reason alone it would be totally useless.* (p. 89; emphasis added)

Such was Clausewitz's conclusion. It would be a good place for any contemporary strategic thinker to begin.

Further reading

The translation by Michael Howard and Peter Paret used in this study, *Clausewitz On War* (Princeton, 1976), is based on the first edition of 1832. Earlier translations had used later and corrupt editions: that by J. J. Graham, first published in London in 1873 and reissued with an introduction by F. N. Maude in 1908, and that by O. J. Mathijs Jolles (New York, 1943). A truncated edition of the Graham translation was published by Penguin Books in 1968 with an introduction by Anatole Rapoport, but the declared intention of the editor to offer only 'those portions of *On War* which relate most directly to our own time' resulted in serious omissions and distortions of Clausewitz's thought.

Those who can read no language other than English need, and indeed can, look no further than Professor Peter Paret's *Clausewitz and the State* (OUP, 1976), an authoritative biography and a comprehensive study of Clausewitz's thought that rendered all previous studies in any language out of date. This can now be supplemented by Azar Gat, *The Origins of Military Thought from the Enlightenment to Clausewitz* (OUP, 1989), which sets his thinking in a broader context. Professor Paret, with Daniel Moran, has also published a selection of Clausewitz's *Historical and Political Writings* (Princeton, 1992). Another comprehensive survey of Clausewitz's thought and influence by a non-German scholar is Raymond Aron, *Penser la guerre, Clausewitz* (2 vols., Paris, 1976, which, although translated into English as *Clausewitz, Philosopher of War*

(London, 1983), is best read in the original. A valuable analysis of Clausewitz's reception in the English-speaking world is Christopher Bassford, *Clausewitz in English: The Reception of Clausewitz in Britain and America 1815–1945* (OUP, 1994). A more general survey to be highly recommended is Michael Handel (ed.), *Clausewitz and Modern Strategy* (Frank Cass, 1986).

Apart from these, all serious studies have been in German, and Professor Paret provided a guide in a comprehensive bibliographical survey in *World Politics*, 18/2 (Jan. 1965). All earlier editions of On *War* were displaced by that of Professor Werner Hahlweg, *Vom Kriege* (Berlin, 1952), which has since been frequently updated. Professor Hahlweg has also brought together a number of lesser works in *Carl von Clausewitz, Verstreute Kleine Schriften* (Osnabrück, 1979). The most comprehensive recent study is that by Wilhelm von Schramm, *Clausewitz, Leben und Werk* (Esslingen, 1977). Although some of Clausewitz's campaign studies, especially that of 1812, have been translated into English, no comprehensive edition of his works has as yet been produced.

Index

Clausewitz

Visit the
VERY SHORT
INTRODUCTIONS
Web site

www.oup.co.uk/vsi

➤ **Information** about all published titles

➤ News of **forthcoming books**

➤ **Extracts** from the books, including titles
not yet published

➤ **Reviews** and views

➤ **Links** to other **web sites** and main
OUP web page

➤ Information about **VSIs in translation**

➤ **Contact** the editors

➤ **Order** other **VSIs** on-line